READY
for COLLEGE

READY
for COLLEGE
everything you need to know

MICHAEL FRANCIS PENNOCK

SORIN BOOKS   Notre Dame, Indiana

www.avemariapress.com

International Standard Book Number: 1-893732-92-4

Cover and text design by Brian C. Conley

Printed and bound in the United States of America.

Library of Congress Cataloging-in-Publication Data
    Pennock, Michael.
        Ready for college : everything you need to know / Michael Francis Pennock.
            p. cm.
        Rev. ed. of: Off to college. c1997.
        Includes bibliographical references.
        ISBN 1-893732-92-4 (pbk.)
        1. College student orientation—United States. 2. College students—Religious life—United States. I. Pennock, Michael. Off to college. II. Title.

    LB2343.32.P455 2005
    378.1'98—dc22

                                                          2004020864
                                                          CIP

Acknowledgements

Again, for the second edition of this book, I wish to thank the hundreds of former students who have written me from college over the years. Their trust in my advice has given me the confidence to write this book and update it for future beginning college students.

My heartfelt gratitude goes out in a special way to my daughter, Amy, and her friends, Lisa Watson and Therese Schindler; my son, Christopher; and my wife, Carol, whose contributions and suggestions were invaluable.

Thanks, too, to former students, Lou Garcia, Brian Tomcik, Dan O'Malley, and Brian Trafis. They generously reported the ups and downs of their first months away at college.

I also wish to acknowledge the contributions of my friend and colleague, Paul Prokop, for his artwork. He is a fantastic teacher, Christian father and husband, and an outstanding witness to the faith. I also wish to thank Fr. Bob Welsh, S.J., former President of St. Ignatius High School, who originally suggested that I write this book; and Fr. Tim Kesicki, S.J., current president of St. Ignatius, who granted me a sabbatical year to work on my writing. I am indebted to these two Jesuits and so many other members of the Society of Jesus for their many kindnesses to me over the years.

Finally, I wish to acknowledge the outstanding contributions of my editor, Mike Amodei. His gentle manner and enthusiastic support have inspired and encouraged me.

I am truly blessed and wish to thank the Lord and pray that this book will help its readers survive the first year of college.

Contents

HIGH SCHOOL VS. COLLEGE

- In high school, you live with your parents. In college, you live with your friends.
- In high school, it never took two weeks to get money from Mom and Dad.
- In high school, a ten-page term paper was a bear; in college, it is a gift.
- In college, there is no one to tell you not to eat pizza three meals a day.
- In college, weekends start on Thursday.
- In college, when you miss class, you won't need a note from Mom reporting that you were cutting, that is, taking a "mental health" day.

TRUTHS YOU'LL LEARN IN COLLEGE

- You can't live without e-mail.
- Quarters are worth their weight in gold.
- Care packages from home rank up there with Christmas.
- Going to bed by 2 a.m. is an early night.
- People you thought were nerds in high school are okay now.
- There are a lot of people smarter than you; there are a lot of people dumber than you.
- There is a direct correlation between alcohol consumption and a low GPA.
- Your life will change for the better . . . or worse. Truth is, you'll never be the same.

Congratulations on your impending or just celebrated high-school graduation! An important phase of your life is over, and now you are ready for COLLEGE. There are lots of things to learn, some of which are listed on the previous page.

If you are like most people, you have many questions concerning the future that will unfold for you in just a short time:

- Will I ever decide on a major, let alone a career?
- How will the coursework be?
- Can I handle the inevitable pressures of drinking and partying?
- How hard will it be to make new friends?
- Will I get along with my roommate?
- How will I keep in touch with my high school friends, including my girl/boyfriend?
- Will I be homesick?
- Will I still go to church if no one makes me?

But think back. Not too long ago you were a *high school* freshman with a host of worries and anxieties as you began that chapter of your life. And you survived! Your only question now is "Where did the four years go?"

My hope and prayer is that this new edition of *Ready for College* will help you survive the next few months of your new life. In writing it, I drew on my own experience as a college student and as a college instructor. I also learned from the experiences of my four children, all of whom have successfully weathered the storms and stresses of college life. (Sometimes they took their dad's advice and sometimes not.) But most importantly, this book has drawn its inspiration from the nearly 12,000 college-bound students I have been privileged to teach in thirty-six years of teaching high school theology. Once in college, many of these students have written letters (and in recent years, sent a steady stream of e-mails), phoned (sometimes in the wee hours of the morning), or stopped by at school or my home to share their victories, setbacks, and dreams, or simply to ask for advice on how to handle some problems they were having.

A government report estimates that over half of all four-year college entrants (in excess of 600,000 students per year) leave without getting degrees.[1] Most students who drop out of college do so between their freshman and sophomore years.[2] As loving parents, my wife Carol and I always wished we could give a simple handbook to our children to help them survive their first months of college—the most critical of the entire time at college, in my judgment. Because I have also looked upon my students as lifelong friends, I also wanted to share survival tips with them. Finally, after years of giving a college survival pep talk to my graduating seniors the last day of class, I wrote the first edition of this book, a compendium of practical ideas and hints to help a freshman make it through the first months of college.

This second edition of *Ready for College* still includes pointers to help you cope with varied aspects of your college experience, from dealing with a troublesome roommate, to managing your health, to defending your religious beliefs before an insulting professor. It updates some of the new challenges of college life and provides new help based on recent research findings, technological advances, and the experiences of my former students, including my son, Christopher, and his friends, recent graduates from college.

As you go off to college, my prayers and blessings are with you.

Counting Down the Days

Your minds, then, must be sober and ready for action.
—1 Peter 1:13

TOP REASONS COLLEGE STUDENTS DROP OUT

1. Too much fun paid for by skipping classes and not studying
2. Homesickness; feeling alone
3. Not prepared academically
4. Not enough money
5. Family issues
6. Lack of academic fit
7. Wrong major
8. Lack of advising
9. Demands of employment
10. Geographic relocation[1]

Think back to this past year with all its stress and the tension of gaining acceptance to college, the destiny of about two-thirds of today's high-school graduates. Perhaps you took the SAT three times, the ACT twice, rewrote college essays until you were cross-eyed, begged teachers for letters of recommendation, and visited so many colleges that you reached the point where you could not tell what state you were in. As you look back, you might ask yourself what does it all mean in the cosmic scheme of things?

If you got into the college of your choice, that's wonderful. Congratulations! But if you didn't, has the world ended? Many who are rejected by their first choice often get depressed. They judge themselves to be second-class citizens compared to their classmates, the real "winners" in the high-stakes contest of college admission.

However, a word of advice: Have no regrets. You got into college! And it was one that was definitely on your list of preferred schools or you would not have applied in the first place. *You* deserve congratulations, too.

One of the important life lessons I have learned is that if you are a good person who honestly gave your utmost effort in pursuit of a worthy goal (for example, trying to get into your *ideal* college), and the door was closed to you, consider that God might have something else in mind for you. Imagine the very real possibility that the college you are about to enter has some great surprises in store for you. Perhaps you will meet your future husband or wife there. Or you may run into a dynamic professor who will turn you on to her subject matter and a career option that will bring you great happiness in life. It is also highly likely that you will meet some like-minded, caring individuals who will become lifelong friends. Perhaps your faith will grow even deeper as you cultivate a profound friendship with Jesus Christ and learn to examine more maturely and then stand firm in your beliefs.

A recent student of mine shared this story with me before his graduation. In early April, he and his classmates had just finished a class in which I asked them to check out the various gospel chapters and verses that corresponded to their birthdays. For example, if a birthday fell on June 7, they were to look up chapter six, verse seven in all the gospels and then choose an appropriate verse that meant something to them. (If the verse was not meaningful, I asked them to look in one of the Pauline epistles instead.)

Of the gospel verses that corresponded to this young man's March 17 birthday (3:17), my student chose Matthew 3:17, "This is my beloved son, with whom I am well pleased." As it turned out, that night, he received a rejection letter from a top notch Catholic university, a school he had been dreaming about going to since he was a small boy. However, instead of being disheartened, he took great solace in the verse that he had reflected on earlier in the day. What was important to him was not that he got into the school of *his* heart's desire, but that *he* was a beloved child of God.

Incidentally, my former student goes to another great Catholic college and is supremely happy there, positive that the Lord led him to an even better choice.

You know, what is true of this student is also true of you. You are God's beloved child—whether you go to an Ivy League college or to the local community college. To put it bluntly, who really cares *where* you go to college? Once you are out in the "real" world, almost no one asks what school you went to. And, surprise of surprises, no one is much interested in your GPA, either. In contrast, people are interested in what kind of person you are, whether or not you shine at your job or career, whether you have developed your talents and use them to create a fulfilling life for yourself and others.

The question now is not *what* school you are going to, but *why* are you going to school.

Why Go to College?

Having a reason for doing something can be a powerful motivator to keep you on course. Having a good reason for going to college, and then doggedly following your course, will more likely lead to success.

What is the purpose of a college education? Kenneth L. Woodward, a senior writer for *Newsweek* magazine and a graduate of my high school, believes there are three related questions an undergraduate education should force you to face.

- What is worth doing?
- What would I like to do?
- What can I do, given my limitations?[2]

Are these your questions as you set off to college? Are you trying to find out what is worth doing, that is, discovering what is the "good life," as the philosopher Plato asked. Do you already know what you want to do, or are you like most entering freshman that classify themselves as "undecided"? And what are you good at? Have you *really* discovered all your potential, or do you need more challenges to teach you about your untapped gifts?

Ideally, you are going to college for lofty motives like those defined by your answers to the three questions above. But in reality, many students go to college for various other reasons: because their parents expect it, for job training, to prepare for a high-paying career, to meet new people (including a future spouse), to learn independence, because their friends are going, and, lest we forget, "to party." For some, the bottom line is simple: It is financially worthwhile to go to college. For example, it is estimated that male college graduates earn 60 percent more than their counterparts with only a high-school diploma. Female college grads earn 90 percent more.[3] In tough economic times, these statistics might be motivation enough.

Now is the time to pause and take stock. Why are *you* going to college? What really motivates you to embark on this new adventure? Here is a short list of possible reasons. How many apply to you? Be honest in your assessment.

I am going to college to . . .

have fun	find out more about myself
prepare for a career	prepare for life
learn how to increase my earning power	grow in my Christian faith and practice
be with my old friends	learn how to learn
keep my parents happy	make new friends
find a spouse	look good in others' eyes
become a contributing member of society	get away from home
reach my potential	

Most people have mixed motives for whatever they do. That's okay. However, one thing you will discover is that college involves a lot more work than high school. You will more likely find the effort worth it if you have some solid reasons for doing it. Having a worthwhile purpose for going to college will see you through the tough times.

Will I Succeed?

"Success is a journey, not a destination."
—ANONYMOUS

"If someone had told me I was going to be pope one day,

I would have studied harder."
—POPE JOHN PAUL I

How did people react to you when you told them you were going to college? Perhaps your guidance counselor said, "You'd better maintain that GPA."

Then, when you *did* get accepted into a good college, maybe a negative-thinking math teacher remarked, "Just wait. It's not going to be as easy as you think."

Or possibly a cynical classmate said, "How did you ever make it? You must have an uncle in the registrar's office!"

Every new college student I've ever known has had a lingering doubt about whether or not he or she will make it through the freshman year. For example, I met an outstanding former student of mine one month before he began his freshman year at the University of Notre Dame. He said that he was excited about going, but that he was a bit jittery about whether or not he could cut it. Time has proven that he has been able to "cut it," and so, too, will you. To do so, keep some basic affirmations in mind, the most important of which is this truth: YOU WILL SUCCEED!

> **If at first you don't succeed, skydiving is not for you.**

First off, statistics are on your side. A friend of mine is the director of admissions at a Jesuit college. A few years back, I petitioned him to accept a student of mine. In our discussion about whether my student would be successful or not, he said that colleges today accept *only* those students who have the academic credentials and study habits to master their programs. If students flunk out, it doesn't reflect well on either the admissions department or the college in general. As noted above, most college drop-out rates have to do with factors other than not being prepared academically.

The mere fact that your college accepted you is, then, a strong vote of confidence that you will succeed. You will fit in, adjust to the new environment, make friends, and handle the work. The college believes in you. So there is no reason not to believe in yourself as well. Make up your mind to work hard from the day you set foot on campus and within a month's time you'll know that you can manage the program.

Exactly what does it mean to be successful? Robert Collier said, "Success is the sum of small efforts, repeated day in and day out." Contrast that wise saying with the comic W.C. Fields who stated, "If at first you don't succeed, try, and try again. Then give up. There's no sense in being a damned fool about it."[4]

What criteria will *you* use to judge yourself a successful college student? Success, like happiness, is elusive. The more you chase it, the more it seems just out of your grasp. Instead, think of success as a by-product of your own inner vision and hard work.

One truth is clear: don't allow anyone else to define success for you. A common ploy is for others to get you to measure up to their ideas of success. In the popular media, for example, a "successful" person is anyone who is filthy rich, drop-dead gorgeous, socially powerful, athletically superior, or all of the above. If you believe in these labels, and then don't achieve them, you may consider yourself a failure. But note: How others define success may not be right for you, or for anyone else for that matter. As a wise person once said, "If you wish to be like someone else, you waste the person you are."

Apply these false notions of success to Jesus, for example. According to the worldly criteria, Jesus was a total failure. He certainly wasn't rich, materially well-off, or powerful. He wasn't even very good at keeping friends. Look what his friends did once he was arrested. They fled, and the one he appointed leader—Peter—even denied knowing him. Blessed Mother Teresa of Calcutta said that at judgment time Jesus won't be asking how successful we were. He will only be asking if we were faithful.

One good strategy for determining success is to reject labels others put on you. Your job, clothes, hobbies, possessions, athletic skills, friends, or GPA are not *you*. Rather, you are a unique person. Stop playing the comparison game of judging yourself according to others' looks, brains, wealth, accomplishment. This exercise in futility will only lead to a poor self-image. Set your own high Christian standards, in line with those of your loving family, and measure yourself against those.

In *Happiness Is an Inside Job*,[6] John Powell writes that happiness, or success, is something within the human heart and not something external; an "inside job" if you will. He tells us that we cannot directly pursue success because it is a byproduct of living a good, wholesome, involved life.

Powell lists ten practices that he believes we must do to have a successful and happy life. I restate them below with a reflection or two that I hope will help you manage your first months in college. By the way, *Happiness Is an Inside Job* would be a terrific book to read before going off to college. The ten practices are:

1. **Accept yourself as you are**. List your strengths and weaknesses in all aspects of your life: mental, physical, and emotional.

2. **Accept full responsibility for your life.** Do you believe that it is in your power to succeed in college? Blaming others or external factors is usually pointless.

3. **Fulfill your needs for relaxation, exercise, and nourishment.** Chapter 5 offers some practical ways to do this.

4. **Make your life an act of love.** Are you committed to loving other people in a Christian sense? Do you love yourself in a healthy way? How do you continue to show your love for God?

5. **Stretch out of your comfort zone.** As you begin college, why not try something new and challenging?

6. **Learn to be a good-finder.** Good-finders look for good in themselves, others, and all situations in life. Are you a good-finder? Can you find something "good" in a recent setback?

7. **Seek growth, not perfection.** Very few people can achieve perfect grades. But you can aim high. And if you don't achieve your goal, you will grow for having tried. What will you strive for? Remember there are three kinds of people: those who make things happen, those who watch what is happening, and those who don't know what's happening.

8. **Learn to communicate effectively.** Sharing your thoughts and feelings with others, as well as listening, will help you make and

keep friends. Do you want someone to get to know you well during your freshman year? Are you willing to listen to others—with your ears *and* your heart? Chapter 2 discusses ways to communicate effectively.

9. **Learn to enjoy the good things in life.** What hobby or activity brings you enjoyment? Can you continue to pursue it in college? Will you?

10. **Make prayer a part or your daily life.** Prayer will help you be a successful college student (see Chapter 5). It will calm you, assure you of God's love and acceptance (despite personal setbacks), inspire and energize you, and help you keep everything in perspective. It's okay to pray for success.

Review and practice these suggestions before you start college. They will go a long way to help you be a successful, happy, self-directed, and loving person . . . and a great student!

5 WAYS TO UNHAPPINESS

1. Compare yourself to others. A sure path to misery.
2. Be a perfectionist. You'll never make it. Criticize yourself for falling short.
3. Sweat the little stuff. Make mountains out of molehills and you'll never get over them.
4. Worry about everything. It leads to anxiety, a true happiness killer.
5. Love things; use people.

Set Realistic Goals

"Show me a satisfied person and I will show you a failure."
—Thomas Edison

Goal-setting and success in college go hand-in-hand. Consider the warning of Yogi Berra, the Yankees' Hall of Fame catcher: "You have to be very careful if you don't know where you are going, because you might not get there." If you can make sense of that quote, then you know the value of setting goals and working to achieve them! Setting goals for your freshman year is worthwhile and something you should do before you go off to college. Here are four goal-setting tips:

1. *Set specific, measurable goals.* You want to graduate with honors. Then, state this clearly rather than simply saying "I wish to do well." Instead, you must ask, "What specific steps will I take during my freshman year to achieve this goal?"

2. *Be sure to set goals for immediate future.* It's okay to aim for admission to medical school, but be sure to set a goal to get an "A" in the required pre-med biology course during your first semester. (Part of core courses like biology are meant to separate the unfocussed and uncommitted students from those who are really committed to pay the price of admission to medical school.) To get that "A" may require setting the additional goal of studying an extra three hours every Saturday afternoon. And possibly Sunday afternoon, too!

3. *Don't be a slave to your goals.* Life is full of surprises. An old truism goes, "If you want to make God laugh, tell him *your* plans." God may have an entirely different life agenda in mind for you. I know this was true for me. I entered college planning to go to law school, but became a teacher and writer instead. Think of your goals as *guidelines* that inspire you to action. But pursue them humbly in case the Lord has other plans for you.

4. *Set your own goals.* College is a time for you to become your own person, to live responsibly and lovingly, setting and working to attain your own goals.

Herbert Bayard Swope maintains, "I can't give you a sure-fire formula for success, but I can give you a formula for failure: try to please everyone all the time." Capable people are *self*-determining. They do what *they* think is right. They set their own goals. Psychologist Fritz Perls adds, "I did not come into this world to live up to your expectations. And you did not come into the world to live up to mine." By the way, one week before my high school graduation, a teacher told me not to expect to do as well academically in college as I had in high school. I took his comments as a personal challenge and made it my goal to do better in college. And I actually did do better. By graduation, I was near the top of my class!

Act Now: Write ten specific and realistic goals you want to achieve during your first months in college. Include personal, social, and academic goals. Here are several examples:

Personal: I will continue to exercise. One way I will do this is to join an intramural sport.

Social: I will join a club and participate in dorm activities to widen my circle of friends.

Academic: I will attend *all* classes.

The Summer Before

*Honor your father and your mother, that you have a long life
in the land which the Lord, your God, is giving you.*
—EXODUS 20:12

The two or three months before college can be a stormy time, and I don't mean rain! Your relationship with your parents is changing, and it's important to proceed carefully in dealing with your mom and dad. Here are some issues you will most surely face:

You and the 3 "I's"

You are moving from adolescence to young adulthood. In psychological terms, this transitional period is a time of searching for *identity*, *independence*, and *intimacy*. It is filled with great expectation, hope, and anticipation. It is normal for you to want to be your own person. . . right now. You want to discover for yourself who you are apart from your parents as well as your siblings and high school friends. You are anxious to begin a more independent life where you decide for yourself and set your own agenda. You want to deepen friendships with others who love you for who you are. And you want to do all these *immediately*, though you are still living at home under your parents' authority and rule.

Mom and Dad: Letting Go Is Tough

Seeing their children go off to college is stressful for most parents. Intellectually, they know you have grown up and it is time for you to separate and assert your independence. They really do want you to be self-confident and self-reliant. But emotionally, when they look at you they still see that gap-toothed, knee-bandaged five-year-old they sent off to kindergarten. Listen sometime to the lyrics of "Sunrise, Sunset" from the musical *Fiddler On the Roof*. Then you'll begin to understand the longing your parents have for you and their plaintive lament of your growing up too fast.

FROM *FIDDLER ON THE ROOF*

Tevye: Is this the little girl I carried? Is this the little boy at play?

Golde: I don't remember growing older. When did they?

Tevye: When did she get to be a beauty? When did he grow to be so tall?

Golde: Wasn't it yesterday when they were small?

When you put together your need to make the future happen now with your parents' nostalgia for the past, there is bound to be a certain amount of friction at home in the summer before college. Sometimes when seniors graduate from high school they immediately expect all the freedom they will have once they are away at college: no curfew, no rules, no reporting about one's whereabouts. Parents, on the other hand, are ambivalent about letting go. They know that when their child leaves for college they'll be losing control. This can scare them.

So they sometimes begin to micro-manage the life of their son or daughter in often unrealistic ways. New rules materialize out of nowhere. Overreaction to slight offenses seems like a daily occurrence. Fights about trivial little things begin to occur.

A bit of advice: Be patient with your parents and with yourself. St. Paul was right when he listed patience as the first quality of love in his famous litany on love in 1 Corinthians 13:4. Try your best to conform to your parents' wishes.

Here's a case in point: Perhaps your parents want you to come on a family vacation. This is the last thing you want to do. You have a ton of high-school graduation parties to attend, you need to work the maximum hours to increase your summer earnings, and you really don't want to spend time traipsing around with your younger siblings. But from your parents' point of view, this may be the last time the whole family will be together. They want to hold on to and savor the family unity they have worked so hard to achieve. Here is a case where a good choice on your part is to "bite the bullet" and go along. And you might even have fun and feel a bit nostalgic too.

Understand the turmoil your parents are experiencing. Even if it seems they can't wait for you to get out of the house—especially if you've been difficult—deep down, they don't really want you to leave. Do your best to go along and keep things pleasant at home. Compromise when possible.

Surely, you'll want a good relationship with your folks when you're away at college. The best way to achieve that is to leave a good relationship at home.

Talk It Out . . . Now!

Entrust your works to the Lord, and you will succeed.
—PROVERBS 16:3

A key to maintaining a good relationship with your parents is to keep the lines of communication open. Make time in the weeks before you begin college to discuss four very important topics with your folks: *values, academic expectations, communication,* and *money.* Here is more information about each:

Values

College is a time of separation, independence, thinking on your own, and becoming your own person. You will meet many people who have different values than you or your parents. They will challenge your beliefs and may even tempt you to forsake them.

Your parents know all of this, and they worry. They worry about things that may not seem important to you: like whether you'll get a tattoo or one or more body piercings, change your hair style, wear grubby clothes, forget the cleanliness habits you've learned since you were an infant, and eat only junk food. They also worry about more significant issues: that you might abandon your faith, stop going to church on Sundays, experiment with drugs, abuse alcohol, or engage in promiscuous sex. Remember the definition of a parent: "one who worries . . . often needlessly."

Needless worry or not, your parents care deeply about you. They know that the new environment you are going into might tempt you to leave your Christian values behind. Now is the time to discuss these issues honestly with your parents. Ideally, you can reassure your mom and dad that you will not do anything foolish and that you will engage in only safe and moral behavior. In turn, hopefully your parents will reassure you of their love and support during these crucial years of growth.

Academic Expectations

Remember the main reason you are going to college: to learn and be educated. This education may eventually prepare you for a career, vocation, and job. To attain all of these goals you must go to class, study, take notes, study, read texts, study, do research, study, work problems, study, write papers, study, take tests, and study. And for the privilege of doing all of the above you and your parents will likely pay a lot of money!

Believe it or not, college education is still a privilege, not a right. The state does not guarantee its citizens advanced education. If you want it, you have to pay for it through loans, scholarships, grants, work-study programs, jobs, and good old hard cash . . . lots of it. Most likely, your parents are making significant sacrifices for you to go to college.

Right before you begin college, it is a good idea to openly discuss with your parents your future academic performance and their financial support.

I know parents who tell their children, "I will not pay for D's and F's." I told each of my four children, "I can help you for the equivalent of four years of undergraduate work. Anything beyond that and you are on your own. It would not be fair to your siblings who will also need support." I also know parents who'll stop paying once their son's or daughter's GPA falls below a 3.8. Personally, I think the first two positions are reasonable, but this last one is simply unfair. Parents must know that college is difficult enough. By setting an unrealistic GPA goal, they are only adding unnecessary pressure that contributes to failure.

Communication is important here. Parents need to know that it may take some adjusting before their sterling high-school graduate earns his or her college wings. For example, some college freshmen, sporting a lofty high-school GPA, get off to a disappointing start. Why? It could simply be that their high school was not challenging enough. Research shows that many college freshmen lack the knowledge of the particular study strategies that will enable them to excel in their new learning environment. The college scene puts a premium on personal responsibility (the professors won't nag you to do your homework). It also moves along at a faster pace, demands much more time in personal study, and usually relies on fewer tests and assignments to factor in one's ultimate grade. For the long haul, success in college requires motivation, hard work, and resolve.

If you have a good relationship with your parents, it should be easy to reach a compromise on realistic expectations, especially for the first year as you adjust to the new learning environment. No matter what you agree to, assure your parents that you will always work hard and try your best. And frequently express your appreciation for the sacrifices they are making on your behalf.

Communication

Decide ahead of time how you plan to stay in touch with your parents (and siblings) while you are away at college. Usually this involves making phone calls and exchanging e-mails. Even if you plan to commute, you may want to set aside time from your busy schedule to touch bases with family members to share what's going on in your lives. For those who live away at school, staying in touch is an especially important issue.

Some parents want at least one phone call a week. There are many cell phone billing options that allow a reasonable long distance plan. In fact, it is almost impossible for college students to live without a cell phone these days. You and your roommate(s) will probably also share a phone in your dorm room. Someone should bring an answering machine if your college does not have a call-forwarding or voice mail system in place as part of its dorm package. Check this out ahead of time.

Long-distance phone calls can be very costly if you don't monitor your calls based on non-peak hours as dictated by your calling plan. One of my own children had astronomical bills from out-of-control calls to his girlfriend and us. Needless to say, after we received the first bill some changes were in order, including:

- Have your folks call you at a planned time.
- Write down topics you want to bring up so you don't forget anything.
- If you do the calling, do so when rates are cheapest. Phone plans differ greatly, but it is usually safe to call after 9 p.m. on weekdays, all day Saturday, and before 5 p.m. Sundays.
- Consider getting a cell phone. For young women especially, it might be a good idea to have one for safety reasons. Many cell plans give thousands of "free" minutes on weekends and evenings. Just be sure that you don't call or receive calls during non-peak hours.

Money

A college student sent his parents this message. "In a bad way. No friends. No money. Please help!" His father sent a reply: "Make friends!"

Spending money is another issue to talk about with your mom and dad before beginning your first semester. Like the general population, some students handle money well; others don't have it long enough to get their hands on it. My own children were proof of this. One son always ran out of money and had to borrow frequently to finish the semester. In contrast, one of our daughters saved enough from her college allowance to have a down payment for a car her senior year.

For all college students, though, there is never *enough* money. This next section examines some money survival tips for your freshman year.

Money, Money, Money

"Too many people spend money they haven't earned to buy things they don't want, to impress people they don't like."
—WILL ROGERS

"The lack of money is the root of all evils."
—MARK TWAIN

In regard to the college experience, Mark Twain's tongue-in-cheek rewriting of 1 Timothy 6:10 has some validity. There are rarely enough funds to cover all the expenses of a college education. After the tuition and room and board bills are paid, the cash outlays have just begun.

For example, you'll need textbooks. You will probably be quoted a dollar amount to allocate for texts. Add hundreds of dollars to their estimate. The price of texts has soared in the past two decades—238 percent, while the price of consumer goods rose only 51 percent. A chemistry book today can cost close to $200![7] As a cost-saving measure, buy used books whenever possible. Be sure they are relatively unmarked, with the highlighting not overdone. A second cost-saver: Don't sell the books back to the bookstore. Rather, post a notice in the student center. You'll likely get a higher price. Another option many students are choosing is to buy and sell their books online, either through their campus or apart with clearinghouses such as E-bay and the like.

You'll also need money for supplies (paper, notebooks, pens, computer supplies, etc.), lab fees, and car expenses. If you're living away from home, phone bills, laundry, snacks, stamps, and toiletries will add to your expenses.

If your home is a distance from campus, you'll need money for travel back and forth to school, a major expense. For commuters this involves having and maintaining a car: insurance, gas, oil, parking passes, and repairs. If you live on campus, money to travel is a major consideration. Money-savers for getting you and your belongings to and from school include sharing with other students the cost of car rides and trailers and trucks for shipment of your belongings. Seek savings on airfare through searches on-line for the best fares. This usually involves purchasing tickets well in advance.

PLANNING TIPS

- Look into a frequent flyer program to and from the city of your college. Some credit cards give bonus miles credited to certain airlines. This might be a great way to get a free ticket home at least once during your college career.
- Always book your return ticket as part of the roundtrip ticket to school.

Remember, too, you'll need cash for dates, parties, movies, sporting events, and other forms of entertainment.

Finally, be aware of one-time hidden costs that hit freshmen especially hard: a carpet, fan, desk or bed lamp, and small refrigerator for your dorm room. Consider buying some of these items used. Also try to share some of these expenses with a roommate. Depending on your situation, you may also be buying a computer and printer. These are high-ticket items, but well worth the investment. (See page 36 for more information about computers.)

A key to financial survival your freshman year is making budgeting a top priority. Here are some more tips in key financial areas.

Checking Accounts

Many banks today offer free student checking accounts with no monthly maintenance fees, minimum balance requirements, or per-check fees or limits. Though these accounts don't typically pay interest, they are a great bargain for the typical college student. If you're living away from home, open a checking account in the surrounding area of your college so you can easily cash checks and pay by check at the stores near campus.

ATM and Debit Cards

Get *automated teller machine cards (ATM) and debit cards* tied into your checking account. You should be able to get free cards. Most banks do not charge retail transaction fees at their network of ATMs. The smart thing to do is to check out what ATMs are available at your college and open a checking account with the bank connected to that machine. Always check out what withdrawal fees are for the ATM you plan to use. I know a student who racked up a $2 service charge with nearly every $20 withdrawal on his ATM card. His bank charged for every ATM withdrawal not made at one of its own branches.

Always keep your receipts when you withdraw money or make a purchase with your debit card. Be sure to subtract the amount from your checking account balance. Also, remember to never write your PIN number down and put it in your wallet or purse. Keep the bank's toll-free phone number handy in case you lose your card. Most importantly, always make ATM withdrawals in a safe place. Avoid using ATM sites at night or in isolated places.

Credit Cards

Beware! Banks throw credit card offers at you with all kinds of incentives to take them up on their offer. They want to hook you with the "buy now, pay later" dream, or more accurately, scheme. Credit card companies downplay their usurious interest rates on unpaid balances. Furthermore, they know if you run the card up to its maximum, and you can't pay, your folks will probably bail you out.

Carol A. Carolan of the Center for Student Credit Card Education warned of life-altering consequences of excessive credit-card debt for college students.[8] These include leaving school, defaulting on student loans, damaging a credit rating, or even the threat of personal bankruptcy. Furthermore, she cited how credit-card debt causes psychological depression in some students and can add to a lower GPA and increased substance abuse.

Should you get a credit card or not? A recent study found that 83 percent of college students do. Those credit card holders graduate with an average credit-card debt of $2,300 and a combined college loan and credit-card debt of about $20,400![9]

Chances are you will sign up for a credit card, but before doing so, discuss it with your mom and dad. Some good tips include getting only one credit card. Cap your credit limit, perhaps at an amount that would take care of any emergency should it arise (for example, the need to get a plane ticket home). Beware of interest rate promotions. A low initial rate often quickly balloons to 18 percent or more. *Always pay off your credit card balance in full.* This will require a commitment to live within your means.

Credit cards do have many advantages. They are convenient, safe, easily replaced if stolen, and good when traveling or for emergencies. Furthermore, credit card companies usually back up the purchaser in a dispute with a vendor. Credit cards can also help you cash checks, get emergency cash through an ATM, and help establish credit.

Balance these good qualities against the tendency to use credit cards for impulse buying. One estimate holds that people with credit cards spend about one-third more than they would if they didn't have one. A wiser choice is to buy only what you can pay for. For example, you don't *have* to go out to costly clubs and the movies every weekend, especially when your campus has many free events. Finally, unless you are completely independent from your parents' financing, you should always discuss large purchases with your folks to get their input.

To summarize, unless your family has won the multi-state lottery, you must learn to budget your money. Now is a good time to work with your parents to create a realistic budget for your first semester. Use these two charts to plan:

Monthly Budgets	Amount
Fees	
Travel	
Texts	
Supplies	
Local transportation	
Room/cell phones	
Clothing	
Laundry	
Toiletries	
Snack food	
Recreation (movies, music, etc.)	
Emergencies/miscellaneous	
Other:	
Total:	

One-time First Year Costs	Amount
Bike	
Loft (if you decide to build one)	
Refrigerator	
Carpet	
Bed/desk lamp	
Fan	
Computer	
Printer	
Microwave oven	
Other:	
Total:	

What do you think? Is this a realistic figure? Verify each item with at least three college sophomores you know. Ask them to name any unanticipated expenses that cropped up during their own freshman years. Revise your estimated budget accordingly. Then plan to stick to it.

Freshman Orientation

"Perhaps the most valuable result of all education is the ability to make yourself do the thing you have to do when it has to be done, whether you like it or not."
—ALDOUS HUXLEY

"An education isn't how much you have committed to memory, or even how much you know. It's being able to differentiate between what you know and what you don't."
—ANATOLE FRANCE

Colleges vary greatly on how they handle freshman orientation. Some colleges hold a grand orientation week or long weekend for all freshmen (and oftentimes their parents, too) before the term begins. Other colleges have groups of freshmen come in for two or three days throughout the summer for orientation and registration. Still others handle parts of the orientation through "snail mail" or over the Internet with campus meetings taking place at a later date.

Typically, freshman orientation sessions are designed to help you:

- learn what the college expects of you both in and out of the classroom;
- become familiar with the college campus and its many offerings;
- meet other new students;
- take placement exams;
- meet with academic advisors to learn about your major if you have chosen one;
- take care of college business like financial aid, health forms, ID cards, etc.;
- register for courses for the fall term.

Orientations can be intense days of meetings and tours. They typically involve many icebreakers and socials and immerse you into what your particular college has to offer. Online orientation is also becoming increasingly more common. Some colleges allow students to take placement exams, download vaccination forms, buy books, check out dorm rooms, and meet roommates online.

This book is geared for success during your first semester, so a very strong recommendation is for you to pick an early orientation session if you are given that choice. More importantly, *register for courses as soon as you are able to.* The advantage here is for you to have the pick of the courses you want and need before any of them close. Choosing classes can be challenging for first-time college students who are not aware of the difficulty of certain professors or specific courses. Here are some other important tips that have helped my own children and many of my former students:

- Ask around among upper class students about the professors of the courses you are considering. What is required in a particular course? How does the professor rate as a lecturer? When in doubt, it is always best to choose recommended profs over courses that "seem" appealing.
- Register for an extra course with the full intention of dropping the one you like least sometime in the first or second week of the semester. It is always easier to drop a course (even if you are charged a fee) than to add one after the term begins.
- Don't overload with hours your first semester in college. Fifteen or sixteen credit hours are plenty. Many colleges require one of your courses to be a Freshmen Seminar. This makes choosing a little easier. Also, balancing one reading intensive course with a math or a science course is also a wise choice. Generally, you should not take more than one lab course your first semester.
- Most colleges require a core of courses for all undergrads, regardless of major. Other courses are prerequisites that you may have to take depending upon your high-school program, SAT or ACT scores, or placement exams. Besides your required Freshman Seminar, it is probably a good idea to register for a couple of your core courses your first semester. Sample a variety of subject areas. Distribute your choices between one tough course, one easy course, and one or two moderately difficult ones based on your interests and skills. Core courses can serve as a foundation on which to build, especially if you have yet to choose a major.
- If a particular core area is one that you hate, or had a tough time with in high school, don't take it first semester. You need

a successful first year. By waiting, you'll have time to check out an ideal prof to get you through the "dreaded" requirement. **Suggestion**: Consider taking this difficult requirement at a community college and have the credit transferred to your college's program. Depending on your work schedule the summer before you go off to college, you might consider taking it then.

- If you are fortunate enough to enter college with considerable Advanced Placement credit, don't overload on upper division courses your first semester. You need to have some experience with courses at your college before you jump into a bunch of advanced courses. Even the brightest students need time to adjust to full-time college life.

- Decide if you learn best in the morning or afternoon. This is not an automatic decision. Even though you may believe you learn better later in the day, studies have proven that learners retain knowledge best in morning hours. Besides, coming from high school, you are used to being in class in the morning. However, true night owls should probably not sign up for 8:00 a.m. classes. Pick courses accordingly. You might even consider taking an evening course that meets once a week. This will free some study time during the day. My son took this advice and found that his professor was more understanding about course requirements for students who enroll in evening classes since some of them have day jobs.

- Choose a schedule that eliminates down time. Better to have three courses in the morning than one at 8:00 a.m., another at noon, and a third at 4:00 p.m. The all-too-human tendency with a schedule like that would be to waste time waiting around for class.

Sometime in the pre-orientation period before arrival on campus, you will be asked about roommate preferences. Many colleges use computer programs to match roommates according to personality traits, work habits, preferences for food and music, sleep patterns, noise tolerance, and other qualities like how much closeness potential roommates desire in each other. *Be honest in what you report about your likes and dislikes. It might help save trouble later.* For example, if second-hand smoke causes you problems, you should make sure to indicate a preference for a non-smoking roommate, even if the college outlaws smoking in dorm rooms. Remember that you want a successful start to your academic career. **Tip**: Choose a quiet, substance-free dorm that reserves many hours in a day for study. You can always visit rowdier friends on their turf and preserve your room for the relatively quiet retreat for study and sleep that you want it to be.

Think of your freshman orientation experience as a golden opportunity to make friends. Research has shown that the most important survival tip for freshman year is to have a reliable friend. So, during orientation, make a point to meet new classmates. Break out of the temptation of just hanging with high-school friends. Participate in the icebreakers and planned activities, even if some of them seem pointless. Concentrate on learning and remembering names of people you meet. Don't be afraid to introduce yourself to new people. Share something about yourself and then take it from there. Also, avoid typical high-school behaviors of aloofness or trying to "act cool."

Finally, your orientation days are a good time to get to know the campus and where some of your classes might meet. Secure a good campus map and get familiar with it. Check the college Web site before orientation and locate several buildings you definitely want to visit while on campus for orientation.

Computers

"To err is human, to really foul things up requires a computer."
—WITH APOLOGIES TO SHAKESPEARE

Most colleges have state-of-the-art computer labs that are readily available for student use at all hours of the day and night. Dorm rooms are wired to the campus network and the World Wide Web. All that's left for you to decide is whether to bring a computer to college or not. My strong recommendation is to do so. Although your college may not require you to own a computer, invariably campus computers and printers will be tied up the week you need them for your term paper, presentation, or research project. It is much more convenient to conduct Internet research and print out reports from your dorm room.

The bottom line is that the cost of owning and transporting a computer is well worth the investment. Here are some tips:

- Check out your college's Information Technology Web site to learn if your school is more PC or Mac friendly and what you will need to do computing from your residence hall (most likely an ethernet card).
- If you own a computer, verify that it is powerful enough for the courses you might be taking, especially in your major. Is your operating system compatible with the campus's Local Area Network's servers? Check your school's technology Web site for answers to this and other questions.

ONLINE RESOURCES

Be sure to explore the campus through your college's Web site now that you have been accepted to the school. Also, check out the various clubs and organizations that are online; e-mail your new roommate; look into buying some required texts; investigate online travel agencies for plane fares (e.g., www.orbitz.com, www.travelocity.com, and www.expedia.com); and explore the new town and state in which your college is located.

- Does your major (for example, engineering) require a special computer? If so, what are its minimum requirements as to speed, memory, hard-drive space, and the like?
- If you will be purchasing a computer, does your college bookstore or tech center have a special deal on computers? A benefit of buying on campus is that you might have better access to service and tips on installation of software than if you bought a computer at your local store or over the Internet.
- In purchasing a computer, weigh the benefits of owning a desktop versus a laptop. Today, laptops are almost as powerful as desktop computers. They have the obvious advantage of portability, so you can take them anywhere on campus, including classrooms for note-taking during lectures. They can also

access the World Wide Web through wireless Internet connections in various buildings and outdoor areas around campus. Furthermore, laptops take up less space on dorm desks and can easily be taken home on vacations. On the downside, laptops are more expensive to buy and repair, easier to steal, not as user-friendly, and tougher to upgrade than desktop computers. Your decision might come down to where you plan to do the vast majority of your computing while on campus and whether or not you have eagle eyes to guard constantly against theft.

- Ask your parents to add your computer to your family insurance policy. Review this policy before you pack up for college to be sure your other belongings are covered while you are at college.
- Be sure to load up your computer with a good virus-protection program with automatic updates.

Part of freshman orientation will be to show you how to handle your e-mail account and access the local network and Internet from your dorm room and other computer stations on campus. You might also learn that some professors expect you to join chat rooms and submit final papers as e-mail attachments. Chances are that by now you have learned how to surf the Internet by using a search engine like Google. A later chapter will briefly discuss plagiarism, a major temptation for today's college students, who have access to all kinds of sources online.

What to Take for the Dorm

"The wise man carries his possessions within him."
—BIAS OF PRIENE

Packing for dorm living will probably be the toughest job you will face in the days before you leave for college. You must strike a balance between transporting everything you own and bare-bones packing that leaves you needing everything once you get to school.

A few preliminaries before checking out the following lists:

- Before tackling the job of packing and transporting big-ticket items like a mini-refrigerator or a carpet for your dorm room, be sure to contact your roommate to see how you can split expenses.
- Check your college's Web site, or carefully read the rules that the Housing Office may have sent to you, to see what items are *not* allowed in dorm rooms. For example, you may not be permitted to have a halogen lamp (a fire hazard) or a microwave oven. (Most dorm floors have microwaves in a central location for student use.) Why cart around something that is not absolutely necessary? You won't believe how small a dorm room is until you actually have to fit all of your stuff into one.
- Consider the wisdom of *not* bringing your TV and VCR or DVD player. Remember that you are going to college to learn, not to watch the latest primetime fare or afternoon soaps. Human nature is weak. Many a freshman has flunked out of college because he or she allowed the TV to become a master. You don't need the added distraction. College dorms provide rec rooms with televisions if you need to "veg out." And you can be sure that many of your dorm mates will have them, too. But it might be a wise idea for you to leave yours at home.

Here are some categories of other items you will need for college. Make decisions based on your own special needs and gender:

Clothing

lots of underwear and socks
T-shirts
jeans, slacks
shirts (long- and short-sleeved)
dresses, skirts, blouses
shorts
sleeping clothes (pajamas or sweats)
shoes (casual and dress)
athletic shoes
sweaters
sweatshirts and sweatpants
blue blazer and tie/good dress
    for interviews and formal occasions
rain gear
sports gear and clothing
jacket, gloves, hats, scarf, boots

Hints: Don't pack a lot of clothes that need dry cleaning or ironing. Depending on where your college is located, you might bring your winter clothes after a visit home in October or after your Thanksgiving break. Mark your name on your clothes.

For Academic Survival

wall calendar
small-size calendar
assignment book/organizer
Bible
good dictionary
thesaurus
manual of writing style
desk supplies: paper, pens, hi-liters,
    ruler, white-out, scissors, tape,
    stapler, notebooks

Room Necessities

computer with ethernet card and cord
    and surge protector
printer
CD/MP3 player
calculator
radio
travel alarm clock
travel iron with automatic shutoff
for the bed:
    pillow and pillowcase
    bedspread/comforter
    mattress pad
    sheets (check college for bed size)
    blankets
refrigerator (check with roommate)
carpet (check with roommate)
microwave (check with roommate and
    college policy)
glasses, mugs, plates, bowls, and eating
    utensils
lamps (desk, floor), clip-on book lights;
    light bulbs
extension cord: 5-plug outlet with surge
    protector
stationery and stamps
address book (electronic or otherwise)
inexpensive camera
posters for walls with sticky tack
message board for door
fan
wastebasket
foot locker or under-the-bed storage
    boxes
duct tape
tools (e.g., screw driver)
optional: Futon or couch for overnight
    guests (check with roommate)

Personal Items

a toiletry kit or small plastic pail
perfume/cologne
toothpaste, toothbrush, floss
contacts, solution, case
cosmetics
soap, deodorant
shaving cream, razor, other toiletries
nail clipper
hair brush, comb
bottle opener
flip-flops to wear in shower
extra clothes hangers
shampoo, conditioner
hair dryer
medicines (band-aids, pain
   relievers, antacids, sunscreen)
   prescription medications
vitamins
laundry bag, detergents,
   fabric softener
big bath towels, washcloths

first aid kit
wastebasket
heavy-duty garbage bags
   (can be used as a laundry bag)

Hint: Check with the college to see if the dorm room has a phone with a call-forwarding system. If so, you will not have to bring a phone or answering machine.

Transportation

bike with sturdy u-lock
backpack

A good way to transport your belongings to and from your dorm is in bundling suitcases. If you forget anything, it can be shipped to you. If it is not a life-and-death item, your parents can bring it to you on their first visit to campus or you can pick it up on a visit home, for example, at Thanksgiving.

By the way, don't bring valuable jewelry, prized possessions, or a great deal of cash. Unfortunately, college students do steal from each other. My son had an expensive mountain bike permanently "borrowed." He told me he wasn't sure if he locked it or not. *A bit of fatherly advice:* "Always lock your bike to some immovable object." And be sure to secure your bike in your dorm room when you come home for vacations. Remember to lock the door.

And Another Thing: More Questions and Suggestions

"Remember; nothing is small in the eyes of God."
—ST. THÉRÈSE OF LISIEUX

The last section of this chapter covers some other commonly asked questions and issues raised by my students about their preparation for and first days of college life.

How do I say "goodbye" to my high-school sweetheart?
Having a serious boyfriend or girlfriend when you go off to college adds strain to an already stressful situation. I know many former students who left college within the first semester of arrival to be near their high-school sweethearts.

To be honest, most high-school relationships unravel when one or both partners go off to college. College presents opportunities to broaden oneself both intellectually and socially. Absence does not always make the heart grow fonder, as college freshman discover the green pastures of many new people to date. And there is really some truth to the adage: out of sight, out of mind.

College is a time of change, both for you and the person you leave behind. At the least, you should give yourself the opportunity to date other people in college. Putting a "No touch, I'm taken" sign on will lead to emotional struggles—guilt when you feel attracted to someone else, confused feelings, frustrating communication problems, and helplessness in trying to keep an *exclusive* long-distance relationship alive.

The summer after high-school graduation is a good time to discuss with your boyfriend or girlfriend the need to go to college with your options open. If your relationship back home is truly the "real thing," neither time nor miles will destroy it. Discuss the situation honestly, but don't make any promises you can't keep.

Certainly, you can keep in touch with your hometown sweetheart. An *occasional* phone call or e-mail is appropriate. Avoid e-mailing and instant messages every day, however. These take time away from studying. Letter writing is a great way to connect on a deeper level. And, if possible, plan to catch up with one another in person during school breaks.

Giving your boyfriend or girlfriend space to develop is beneficial for him or her as well. Grasping too tightly stifles an individual's development and can drive that person away.

However, let's say you ignore all this advice and are determined to remain exclusively loyal to your boyfriend or girlfriend at home. In this case, you must still find a way to have a social life at college or you will miss out on one of its important benefits. Perhaps the solution is to develop some close friendships and commit yourself to socializing in groups. This would be an acceptable compromise that should not jeopardize your relationship with your hometown boyfriend or girlfriend.

Should I bring a car to college?

Unless you are a commuter student, you will make a smart decision if you leave the car at home, even if your college allows freshmen to bring them to campus.

Listen to the sucking sound of money leaving your wallet for gas, insurance, maintenance and car repairs, and the increasingly expensive college parking pass. Having a car is very costly, especially if you are on a modest budget.

Also, realize that you will immediately be Ms. or Mr. Popularity the minute your friends and acquaintances know that you have a car. They will beg you ("just this once") to take them places or let them borrow your car. Good person that you are, it will be hard for you to turn them down as a chauffeur. The time you spend running errands for others could negatively affect your academics.

You could respond, "I can let them *use* my car." But what if they are in an accident? You share in the responsibility. Their insurance policy may not cover accidents in *your* car. Therefore, it will be *your* insurance rates (or those of your parents) that will go through the roof.

It is cheaper, more convenient, more environmentally friendly, and healthier to walk, use a bike, or, if available, use a campus shuttle service.

But if you do bring a car to campus:
- Always lock your car.
- Never leave anything valuable in plain sight in the car.
- If you lend your car to friends, be very clear about your expectations for its use. Make sure *their* insurance policies cover them in your car.

Will I be able to hold a job and keep up with studies?

During your first semester, you should not get a job. Many students will have to work sometime during their college careers. But try at all costs to avoid taking a job while you are still adjusting to a new setting. The first semester of freshman year involves so many changes and stresses that you need to be free to devote all your energy to coping and to becoming a top-notch student. Once you are well versed in the academic routine of college, then you will know what it will take to get good grades and hold down a job. *Hint:* Here is something you can do your first semester if you think you might be working later on. Begin to scout out the types of jobs that might be available in the office of your major. Landing a job near the center of action might be good help for your eventual chosen career.

Should I bring important documents like my financial aid award or leave them at home?

It's probably better to leave most important documents at home. In any case, create a paper and computer file to save your important documents, including:
- financial aid awards;
- loan documents;
- tuition payment receipts;
- academic documents (including ACT and SAT scores, transcripts, letters of recommendation, diplomas, awards);
- job placement documents;
- insurance policies.

Being able to show written documentation of the highlights of your college career will often be required of you. And colleges do make mistakes and will hold up grades if bills are not paid. Being able to document their errors will resolve disputes more quickly.

Include in your file a copy of the college catalog from your first year of college. Even if department requirements in your academic major are later changed, most colleges will allow you to complete your course of study and graduate under the requirements from when you first enrolled at their school.

Keep your birth certificate and passport (if you have one) in a safety deposit box at home or in a bank.

I know college is expensive. What are some things I can do to save money?
For the frugal, there are many money-saving tips that you can try:

- Buy your school and dorm supplies at a discount store, not at the college bookstore where prices are likely higher.
- Take advantage of the free or inexpensive entertainment (including movies and concerts) that take place on campus.
- Limit how much money you withdraw at any one time from your account, especially at ATMs. You'll find a way to spend any extra money in your pocket or purse.
- Use the campus meal plan to your benefit. If your school has a plan where you can sign up for 14, 15, 19, or 21 meals per week, carefully consider which plan is best for you. If you typically skip breakfast, or eat out occasionally, you might not want to sign on for meals that you won't end up eating. (However, note that the difference in cost between the higher and lower number meal plans vary only by a few dollars at most colleges.) If your food service allows it, take an extra piece of fruit to your room to hold you over when you get the munchies. Trips to the vending machines can kill your budget and your waistline.
- Think weekly budget. Calculate how much spending money you have for the week. Divide this amount by seven. This is your daily allowance. If you want more money available for the weekend, deny yourself some goodies during the week. For example, do you really need to buy that $3 magazine that you just as easily can read in the library or on-line? Won't a $3 store-brand bottle of shampoo work just as well as the $8 name-brand?
- Look for coupons. A two-for-one pizza coupon, for example, can give you and your friends a late-night meal for half the cost.
- Avoid parking fines if you drive. Avoid late fees for library materials or movie rentals. Never withdraw money from an ATM that will charge you fees.
- Resist shopping sprees with a vengeance. How great is the temptation to buy what you don't need or want! It is okay to splurge on occasion, but only as a reward for a job well done. Moderation in all things.

How do I do laundry?

You'll know it is time to do laundry if you find yourself wearing your underwear in the shower to get it clean.

Unfortunately, doing your own laundry when you live in a college dorm is a fact of life. It takes time—about ninety minutes—to wash and dry a load. A good bet is to learn from your mom some time the summer before going off to college. Short of that, here are ten tips for doing laundry:

1. Stock up on quarters.
2. Buy some liquid detergent. (Using fabric softeners, dryer sheets, and bleach is too sophisticated for now.)
3. Empty your pockets.
4. If you don't want pink underwear, separate whites from darks.
5. Don't use bleach on colored clothes.
6. Wash reds separately.
7. To be safe, always wash in cold water.
8. Clean out the lint trap in the dryer.
9. Very hot dryers can ruin your clothes.
10. Fold your clothes, or hang them on hangers, immediately after taking them out of the dryer. This will cut down on some of the wrinkles and you will not have to iron your clothes in most cases.

The best time to do laundry is usually very late at night or early morning. Avoid the weekends when everybody else decides to do it. Guard your clothes. Impatient students waiting to use an idle machine have been known to take finished clothes out of the machines. Yours may end up on the floor. A nice piece of clothing may even disappear. Bring a book to read or plan a jog while your clothes are in the wash or dry cycle. Try not to waste the minutes it takes to do your wash.

The First Weeks on Campus

2

The popular author Robert Fulghum wishes he could give a high-school graduating class a speech on what it means to be a "grownup." In it, he would ask the graduates questions like these:

- Could you clean the sink strainer?
- Could you plunge out the toilet?
- Could you clean up babies when they poop and pee?
- Could you wipe runny noses?
- Could you clean ovens and grease traps and roasting pans?
- Could you carry out the garbage?
- Could you bury pets when they get run over in the street?

As Fulghum points out, being an adult involves lots of dirty work.[1]

Going to college is a major step to adulthood because it involves living on your own. Questions like those posed by Fulghum suggest others that are related to the "dirty work" involved in being a college student. For example:

- Could you honestly tell a roommate that certain of his or her habits are driving you crazy?
- Could you accept others who hold different beliefs and values than you?
- Could you admit that you are homesick?

- Could you ask for help when you need it?
- Could you risk rejection by initiating a friendship in a new setting?
- Could you be flexible enough to find a quiet study area, even if it means traipsing across campus?
- Could you commit to the many requirements of joining a campus activity without undermining your other obligations?

Dealing with issues like these in a mature way signals the making of a responsible college student and adult. In this chapter, you will uncover some of the difficulties (a.k.a. "dirty work") confronting the freshman newly arrived on campus, including how to:

- say good-bye to your parents
- get along with your roommate
- survive the jitters of the first few weeks
- deal with homesickness
- make new friends
- appreciate, not reject, differences in people
- determine when and if to join in campus activities

Saying Good-bye to Mom and Dad

"Always Leave Them Laughing When You Say Good-bye."
—A SONG BY GEORGE M. COHAN

After a hectic few weeks packing and saying good-bye to your high-school friends, you will eventually be ready to go to college. Be ready for a whirlwind of activity, a sense of unreality, mass confusion, and lots of new people, places, and experiences. It will be normal for you to have mixed feelings about all this. On the one hand, you'll feel excitement about the new experience; on the other, you might be a bit fearful and apprehensive about letting go of the old and familiar.

Part of the "blur" of the first few days at college is saying "good-bye" to your parents. For some newly-arrived freshmen, it is quite normal to want their folks to depart campus as soon as they drop them off. If this describes you, you might even find yourself dropping not-so-subtle hints that they should get going to beat the traffic as soon as your key turns the lock of your dorm room. If so, please don't forget David Russell's wise observation, "The hardest thing in life is to know which bridge to cross and which to burn."

You simply do not wish to burn the bridge of love and friendship that your family has spent a lifetime to build. Often, it is simply a matter of perspective. And your view of your first two weeks on campus differs from that of your parents. Consider:

Your perspective	Your parents' perspective
Saying good-bye to family, friends, hometown sweethearts so you can say "hello" to new friends	Saying good-bye to the child they gave life to not that long ago
Enthusiasm mixed with lots of trepidation	Happiness for son or daughter's new status mixed with some concerns/fears about the unknown
Quick lessons on how to live with a new roommate	Reevaluation of their parental role as their student moves from dependent to independent status
Great desire to test your new-found freedom	Confusion/joy over newfound availability of phone and family car

Being sensitive toward your differing expectations and perspectives can help make saying good-bye to your parents a little less traumatic for all of you.

For example, you might be one of those freshmen who will find it hard to say good-bye. It can be tough to say good-bye to those who have shopped for you, cooked, done your laundry, come to your high-school games and activities, solved your problems, and always been there for you. Arriving on campus can be a major dose of reality. So, to delay their parents from leaving too soon, some students invent ploys to keep them around a little longer. For example, they may walk them to the college bookstore to pick up a sweatshirt. Or they might too eagerly jump at their folks' invitation to go out to dinner to a fancy restaurant, even if it means missing an orientation meeting.

Elation over newfound freedom mixed with wariness about letting go is common enough. Going away to college is likely your first real separation from your parents. Thus, ambivalence about assuming new responsibilities, fearing the unknown, and being overwhelmed by the swirl of activity on your day of arrival can make saying good-bye difficult.

Many parents also find it tough to say good-bye after getting their son or daughter moved into the dorm. It is not easy for them to take the big step of leaving their child to the freedom and space that comes with independent living. They know only too well that their relationship with you is changing. Some parents will find this hard to take, especially if you are the first or last of your siblings out of the house. They may be reluctant to let go, to accept that you are growing up and leaving them.

Some parents even resort to behavior that appears irrational. For example, they might insist on setting up your dorm room the way *they* like it. Or they might give last-minute lectures on topics they have already rehashed a thousand times.

Be patient with your parents and with yourself. Here are six general tips on how to handle those last good-byes.

1. Let your mom (or dad) make your bed, organize the clothing in your drawers, or hang up one of your posters. This will help them feel like they put their own stamp on your living space. You can always rearrange your room the way you'd like after they leave for home! Also, you might want to ask your mom or dad some advice on where to put your desk or help with setting up or dismantling a bunk bed or loft.

2. You might have a younger brother or sister who "adores" you and has come along on the trip. If so, lucky you! But know that it may be very tough for them to say good-bye to their hero. Let them help set up your room too. Show them frequent signs of affection. Promise you will e-mail and call them often.

3. Formally introduce your parents to your roommate and your resident advisor (RA). This will help you to establish the tone that accompanies a more mature parent/child relationship.

4. If possible, go to dinner with your folks if this is something they really want to do. This would be a good time to:
   - Thank them for everything.

- Reassure them that you will call or e-mail, weekly at first. (Make sure to follow through with your promise).
- If your college has orientation during move-in week, let them know about any interesting activities that you have experienced so far.
- Invite them to Parents' Weekend (usually six to eight weeks into the first semester). Tell them you genuinely want them (and your siblings) to be there.

5. Walk your parents to the car when they are ready to go home. Leave your roommate and new friends back in the dorm. Share some hugs and kisses and tears—all of which are easier to exchange when strangers are not around. Say what your heart tells you to say. If you find it difficult to do so, write out a letter ahead of time and give it to your folks to read on the way home. They'll love you for your thoughtfulness. But keep it light, too. This is not the permanent farewell known as death; you will see them again.

6. As you return, alone, to your dorm, say a prayer for your parents' safe return home and for the strength to live by the values they have taught you.

Getting Along with Your Roommate

"Be ready to do good at every opportunity; not to go slandering other people but to be peaceable and gentle, and always polite to people of all kinds."
—Titus 3:1–2 (NJB)

It is likely that move-in day may be the first time you will meet your roommate. But if your college provided roommate names during the summer, I hope you were in contact either by phone or e-mail so that your first meeting won't be with a total stranger. Room and hall mates will serve a very important role in your first few months of college as an emotional safety net since they will share many of the same experiences as you. Therefore, getting along with your roommate is a very important part of thriving during your freshmen year.

Here's a good tip: Try to be the first to arrive in your dorm room. With your kind consideration of others, you will be in a good position to compromise on choice of beds, desks, and so forth. A first task you can share with your roommate is to report any room damage that you discover so you don't get charged for it at the end of the semester, something that happened to my daughter and her roommate their freshman year in college. *Hint:* Bring a camera to photograph any damage in your room that you find on arrival.

Because roommates come in all shapes and sizes, you can't assume they will share all of your values. You are bound to have many "What if" questions. Here are some possible ones:

What if my roommate . . .
- abuses alcohol and drugs?
- smokes in the room?
- wants her boyfriend (or his girlfriend) to sleep over?
- steals from me?
- is an exchange student who speaks a different language?
- is of a different race than me?
- is a total slob or a neatness freak?
- always has creepy friends hanging out in our room?
- listens to music that I loathe?
- stays up all night when I'm trying to sleep?
- is a needy, "high-maintenance" person who always wants to talk about his or her problems?
- is gay?

Some of these questions raise real problems; others are not problems at all. A good thing to remember is that your relationship with your roommate can be positive and satisfying, though you are not best friends. You can have different personalities, races, interests, family backgrounds, friends, academic majors, likes and dislikes and still have an honest relationship built on mutual respect. Keep the following suggestions in mind for a positive roommate experience:

1. Have a positive attitude.

   From the very first, expect that you *will* get along with your room-mate. Greet the person warmly when you meet for the first time. Move-in day can induce major stress, especially with all the commotion of moms and dads and siblings and friends moving boxes in and out of your room. You will need a sense of humor and a lot of patience to survive until things quiet down. Keep an open mind about your roommate and suspend judgment based on your first impressions, especially during move-in day.

   At all costs resist *stereotyping* your roommate. Prejudgments made out of ignorance or lack of experience breed fear. Give your roommate a chance. After all, a person's nationality, religion, race, geographic origin, socio-economic condition, or sexual orientation are not bases of condemnation. Your Christian faith asks you to respect everyone as a child of God. Remember: your siblings may not be your closest friends, but you've learned to get along with them. Aim to be congenial, and 99 percent of the time you will have a positive experience with your roommate.

2. Be patient with yourself and your roommate.

   It takes time to get to know another person. Give yourself a chance. Adel Bestavros wisely noted, "Patience with others is love, patience with self is hope, patience with God is faith."[2] Expect a normal amount of tension in your relationship. After all, even brothers and sisters have their stressful moments when living under the same roof.

   Do some activities together the first few days at college; for example, explore the campus or share a meal. Talk about your likes and dislikes. Share stories about your family and high-school experiences. Listen carefully and permit your roommate to share about himself or herself, too.

   A final thought here: If you think that you can change your roommate into an ideal "soulmate," remember how tough it is for you to change yourself. Being patient with your roommate may even lead to a lifelong friendship. And a big payoff for being friends is that the friend can know you, but accept and love you anyhow.

3. Ground your relationship in honest communication.

A key to a successful relationship is honest, gut-level, non-judgmental communication. Practice the art of genuine communication and you'll avoid most potential roommate problems. Within the first week, be sure to discuss the following issues:

- *Borrowing and loaning.* What can your roommate borrow from you without your permission? What personal stuff is "hands off"—clothes, supplies, toiletries (borrowing toothbrushes, for example, is not really healthy!), money, computer, printer, DVD player? To save arguments later, clearly state what you want in this regard and listen to your roommate's preferences, as well.

- *Visiting hours.* What is the dorm curfew for visitors? How will you handle boyfriends or girlfriends? It's best to abide by dorm regulations in this area, since both of you may be held responsible for breaking this rule. It may be touchy to talk about this issue, but it is perfectly okay for you to say that you will not give up your room for an overnight stay of your roommate's friend of the opposite sex. You might as well share your values on this issue up front. If your roommate is gay, apply the same standards. You can do so without being preachy.

- *Sleep.* Are you a night-owl? Do you need your ten hours of sleep, even if it means being in bed by nine? What will bother you (lights, music, the television, visitors) when you're trying to fall asleep?

- *Quiet hours.* Do you expect to study in your dorm room? If so, you should agree to keep some hours sacrosanct for study, for example, from 8:00 p.m. on. Many college students try to avoid early morning classes and routinely go to bed well past midnight. If this describes you or your roommate, then what are your rules for quiet in the morning hours?

- *Space.* How will you divide the space in your room? On which walls will you hang *your* posters? Some roommates like to construct lofts to free up more dorm room. Check your college housing office for regulations. You can purchase loft plans over the Internet (for example, at www.loftworksllc.com).

- *Music and Television.* Share your music preference. Try to agree on an acceptable volume level for whatever kind of music you each like. If you or your roommate brought a television and DVD player, establish a fair-use policy, especially concerning acceptable times to watch.

- *Phone Bills.* Most likely, the phone company will not send out separate bills. You will have to work out a way to divide common charges and assign long distance calls for your in-room phone.
- *Cleanliness.* Are you a neatness freak? Or are you on the sloppy side? How do you plan to keep your space livable? Agree on and assign cleaning chores, just as you might within a family.
- *Smoking and drinking.* Colleges and individual dorms have rules about smoking and drinking in dorm rooms. Make sure to observe them. Also, honestly state your opinion on alcohol, tobacco, and drug use. Many college freshmen who abuse alcohol for the first time (for example, by binge drinking) have been known to vomit. Make a pact that this will never happen in your room, where the offensive odor can linger for the rest of the semester.
- *Confidences.* Just by sharing the same space, you will learn some private details about your roommate's life. How will you handle these "secrets" you learn about each other? Pope John XXIII wrote that true and solid peace among nations came not from arms but from mutual trust alone. How much more will trust between roommates help bring about a peaceful living arrangement.
- *Pet Peeves.* What *really* bothers you? This is your best chance to tell each other of your own idiosyncrasies and habits.

If you agree to be open and honest from your first meeting it will be much easier to gently broach a subject of concern when it arises. Many college students have let things get out of hand because they think problems will go away. They usually don't. Resolve to deal with problems right away instead of letting them simmer. Recall your understanding of the guidelines you agreed to. Always negotiate when you can, but make sure to speak up for your rights, too.

RULES TO KEEP YOUR ROOMMATE HAPPY

1. Know when to take a shower without being asked.
2. Keep wet towels off the beds.
3. Know when and how to ask guests who have overstayed their welcome to leave.
4. Take all phone messages accurately.
5. Get rid of garbage (especially anything that has turned green).
6. Keep your soda drinks and other liquids away from computer keyboards.

---

4. Always show respect.

Remember the golden rule: "Do to others as you would have them do to you." Being considerate and respectful of each other will go a long way to making dorm living a pleasant experience. Simple little courtesies like taking phone messages, respecting your roommate's privacy, and picking up an occasional item for the other while shopping will strengthen a roommate relationship.

Strive to be congenial. You are allowed to be yourself, but remember to allow your roommate the same right. You don't have to be best of friends with your roommate. Each of you can hang out with entirely different sets of friends. But many college students have discovered that their roommate's friends have enlarged their own circle of friends.

5. Don't forget security issues.

Unfortunately, college students are subject to the effects of original sin like any other human being. They steal. Agree to lock your dorm room every time you leave it, even for short trips to the bathroom. If you are going out for a length of time, lock the windows, too. Many a roommate relationship has gone sour when someone forgot to lock the door and the other person had something ripped off.

6. Always be willing to compromise.

An American proverb holds that the more arguments you win, the less friends you will have. Living with another person in close quarters involves compromising with each other. Flexibility is important. Trying to see the other's viewpoint is helpful in reaching mutual understanding.

Most times you will be able to deal with any problems that come up. But sometimes it is tough to resolve your differences. When you reach that point, you might ask your RA to mediate your dispute. Perhaps the RA can help you reach an agreement. A third party can often look at issues more objectively. In more extreme cases, you might even ask the RA to arbitrate your dispute. Arbitration involves agreeing beforehand to abide by the RA's judgment call, whether it favors you or not.

In very rare cases, you might have to request a room change. Perhaps your roommate repeatedly steals your money, is a drug abuser whose behavior is affecting your academic performance, is repeatedly using the room for sexual liaisons, or refuses to compromise on any issue. It is painful to request a room change in the middle of a term, but sometimes it is the only resort. Remember you do have the right to a safe, supportive, and healthy living environment to pursue your education.

Surviving the First Week Jitters

"Nothing in this world can take the place of persistence. Talent will not; nothing is more common than unsuccessful people with talent. Genius will not; unrewarded genius is almost a proverb. Education will not; the world is full of educated derelicts. Persistence and determination alone are omnipotent. The slogan 'press on' has solved and always will solve the problems of the human race."
—PRESIDENT CALVIN COOLIDGE (1872–1933)

You may have heard of future-shock. Prepare yourself for freshman shock! An explosion of activity confronts college freshmen the first few weeks at college. You may find some of the activities, experiences, and people to be scary, overwhelming, and challenging. But others may prod you to peak performance. There is no telling exactly how *you* will react to all the novelty.

First, realize that it is perfectly normal to feel uncomfortable in a new environment. Despite appearances, many of your classmates also are apprehensive.

Second, convince yourself that you will survive the stress of being new to college life. Hang on for a few weeks and you will look back and have a good laugh.

Third, if you run into any of the following situations, don't panic! Try the suggested remedies for each instead.

Hassles with Dorm Living

"Dormitory" comes from a Latin word that means "sleep." As you will soon find out if you live in a college dorm, that is a misnomer. Sleep and dorm-living hardly go hand-in-hand. Living in a dorm is a real eye-opener. Literally.

Perhaps you lucked out and got an ideal roommate (or roommates). But this does not guarantee a spacious dorm room, some of which are the size of broom closets. Then there is the noise! It might seem that everyone on your floor is playing his or her music at full volume . . . 24 hours a day. You quickly learn that your dorm room is not the ideal place to study.

Not only will some floormates constantly party, you may even find pranksters who pull the fire alarm at 3 a.m., rousing everyone from sleep. Then there is food service. College students love to complain about dorm food, and rightly so. How can it possibly measure up to home cooking? Here's what a student wrote to me recently:

> In talking to friends at colleges around the country this first week, one of the questions almost certainly asked is, "How's the food?" A variety of answers are given, but whether it tastes good or not, it almost certainly isn't good for you. I had a serving of meatloaf tonight with nearly a hundred more calories than a Big Mac.[3]

To cope with these inconveniences of college living you should:
- Develop a sense of humor. Living in a dorm requires give-and-take, patience, and the ability to laugh.
- Invest in a Walkman or similar portable music player, earplugs, or even eye shades. There *are* ways to block out noise to get sleep.

- Search for a quiet and safe place on campus to study (for example, a carrel in the library or an empty classroom).
- Make some time for yourself. Jog. Play basketball. Walk around campus. Ride your bike. If your college has a chapel, go for a short visit to meditate. All of these will help you escape the sometimes too hectic pace of dorm living.
- Establish a normal routine. You still need seven to eight hours of sleep. So you must commit to a routine that will get you that amount of sleep so you can still make it to class.
- Keep your refrigerator stocked with healthy snacks (fruits, vegetables, etc.). They are less likely to be snatched by your roommate or other floormates. Remember to hydrate, too, for good health. This means drinking plenty of water, juices, and milk—not caffeinated beverages or beer! This healthy fare will balance the great amount of delivered pizza you are bound to eat. *Hint:* Since pizza is the survival and comfort food of choice for most college students, get the phone number of at least three pizza delivery shops.

Loneliness

Loneliness is the feeling that you are not connected to those around you. It can result in the feeling that no one cares about you. This can happen even in a biology class with 75 other students and you don't know anyone. Or you are the only person from your high school in your dorm (or school) and are feeling lonely and isolated. Or, you are a commuter who notices the "on-campus-people" sticking together and ignoring "outsiders" like you. Unlike high school where you knew everyone, college may seem like a vast wasteland where no one knows your name.

First, realize that loneliness is a common experience for many college freshmen. Being displaced from familiar surroundings is its major cause. It is not a permanent state of affairs and is relatively easy to surmount. Here are some ways to overcome the occasions of loneliness that strike during the first weeks:

- Get to your classes early. Sit in different locations for several days. Immediately strike up a conversation with students who sit near you.
- Be assertive. For example, invite someone from class to meet you for lunch.

- If you commute to campus, find the main spot where the other commuters hang out and socialize. You're bound to meet a kindred spirit there.
- If you live on campus, arrange to eat dinner several times a week (at least) with your roommate.
- Talk to someone in line with you at the bookstore.
- Go to a meeting of a campus activity that interests you. If your schedule can handle it, consider joining up.
- Go to where people are. Study in the library, attend one of the free campus activities, or watch television in the dorm's common areas. You'll be surprised how many people you'll meet, some of whom will actually connect with you.
- Participate in the campus ministry program. Good and caring people work in these types of ministries. Often, retreats and workshops are sponsored where you can meet other people.
- Visit the recreation center. You're likely to find someone who is looking for a pickup basketball game, a spotter in the weight room, a handball opponent, or a companion to swim laps with in the pool.
- E-mail friends at home or on other campuses. Nothing dispels isolation like a stuffed inbox of news from friends.
- Avoid tobacco and alcohol. They will only add to your stress and are not permanent fixes for loneliness.

Study Blues

It's a Thursday night, the third week of the semester. Everyone else is out partying. You are the only one swamped with homework. You begin to wonder: What's going on here? Keep these points in mind:

- If you are working hard, then you are doing the right thing. Good students have accepted the basic truth that almost always guarantees success in college: College is your full-time job. What this means is that *your* main "job" right now is to study. Many freshmen learn this lesson too late. Look for many of the Thursday night revelers to be on the academic probation roll at the end of the first semester. This won't happen to you.
- In fact, you should work even harder to get ahead of your work in a couple of your tougher courses. This may even mean putting in some study hours on a Friday and/or Saturday

night. Then, reward yourself by breaking the routine and joining in with some of the social scene. Learn this lesson early on and you will be a great college student.

Demanding Profs

You are taking an introductory writing course. Included in the course requirements is a weekly essay. You receive a "D" for your first composition. You're very disappointed because the lowest grade you ever received in high school was a "B", and that was in a tough physics course. What do you do next? Consider the following:

- Don't give up. You may have coasted to get an "A" in high school. But remember, this is college, and it *is* tougher than high school.
- Give yourself time to learn and to grow. Many instructors in introductory writing courses assign low grades to start. They are looking for you to improve. And you will improve if you heed their suggestions.
- If possible, move your seat to the front of the classroom. Participate actively by asking questions and taking part in discussions. Many profs will give you the benefit of the doubt if they know you care about their course and are trying to improve.
- Make an appointment to see your instructor to find out in more detail how you can improve. An important study from a Harvard researcher revealed that students who asked for academic help in the freshman year significantly improved their grades compared to those who did not. It is a sign of strength, not weakness, to ask for help.[4]
- Seek out a teacher's assistant (usually upper division or graduate students) for additional help. In the case of a writing course, especially, go to the writing lab for help.

5 THINGS YOU SHOULD RESIST DOING ON THE FIRST DAY OF CLASS

1. Ask whether the assigned reading is mandatory.
2. Ask if class attendance is optional.
3. Sit in the front of the room and fall asleep.
4. As you page through your text, scratch and sniff each picture.
5. Yell "AWESOME!" after every main point made by the professor.

Athletic Setbacks

You had a three handicap as captain of your high-school golf team. But when you try out for the State U. golf team, you don't make it. Positive ways to respond are:

- Don't sweat it. Depending on the college and the sport, competition for a position on a varsity team can be fierce. This does not so much reflect on your talent as to comment on the excellence of the program.
- Most colleges have an active intramural sports program. Sign up to participate in at least one seasonal sport.
- Try a new activity. You'll not only expand your horizons, but you may learn to enjoy it.

Sniffles

What happens when you get sick? Toward the end of your second week on campus you wake up one morning with a sore throat and headache. Mother isn't around to dispense aspirin and her sure-cure chicken soup. Here are some alternative actions:

- Try a recommended over-the-counter medicine, including vitamins. Drink plenty of fluids. Make sure you eat breakfast every day. Be sure to eat healthy foods the rest of the day as part of a well-balanced diet (yes, veggies are important). Check to make sure you are not sleeping in a draft. Dry your hair well before going to bed.

- Make sure you are getting enough sleep, at least seven to eight hours a night.
- If you don't improve in a day or so, visit the school medical clinic. You should especially do so if you have a severe sore throat, pain in the ears or sinuses, a persistent high fever or cough, or trouble breathing. The clinic can check if you have strep throat or some other condition that will respond to a regimen of antibiotics. You need early treatment so you won't miss classes and be sapped of energy for study this early in the term.
- Believe it or not, the best way for you to fight illnesses is to wash your hands frequently with soap and hot water. Because of the close quarters of dorm living, large classes, and eating in cafeterias, you are much more likely to catch a cold or the flu at college than at home. As the saying goes, an ounce of prevention is worth a pound of cure.

Missing Home

"Loneliness is the first thing which
God's eye named not good."
—JOHN MILTON FROM TETRACHORDON (CF. GN 2:18).

I asked a former student, a star high-school and college quarterback with a winning and confident personality, what was the toughest part of his freshman year. He replied, "Homesickness. It took me by surprise how much I would miss my family and friends. I was constantly calling home the first few weeks. But I eventually got over it."

Most freshmen experience homesickness, defined as "a negative emotional response to leaving home." One study revealed that almost 70 percent of freshmen experience it at some time. A counselor at the University of Dayton estimated that up to 90 percent of college freshmen are significantly homesick at one time or another.[5] On the plus side, two-thirds of all homesick students overcame this feeling after one week.[6]

Loneliness, a lack of friends, the stress-filled world of college, a sense of insecurity caused by disorientation in new surroundings—all of these contribute to the very *normal* feelings of homesickness.

Homesickness can be mild in those who have many high-school friends attending school with them or who live close enough to get home to visit when they need to. It is usually more severe in students who are very close to their families, have never been away for any length of time, and who attend a school that is an airplane flight away from home. The worst cases of homesickness result in students transferring schools or dropping out of college. One in four college freshmen does not return for sophomore year. A major reason was a feeling of not being connected, and homesickness had a role to play in these feelings.[7]

There are several ways to survive homesickness. Here are some:

- Remember that homesickness is very natural. It is a normal stage in the process of separating from home and becoming an independent, self-directed adult. The pain will pass, usually sooner rather than later.

- Bring familiar items from home to your dorm room. Posters, photos, and even stuffed animals help you ease into a new environment.

- Be patient with yourself. There is no set schedule for you to adjust perfectly to college. Don't compare yourself to others who appear to have it "together." Many freshmen probably feel like you do but hide behind smiling faces.

- Confront homesickness by taking action. Keep busy. Throw yourself into your studies. This will help distract you from longings for home.

- Make a conscious effort to meet people. Leave your dorm room door open. Study in the library. Introduce yourself to at least one new person each day. Occasionally visit someone from your hometown or high school. Share memories. Most freshmen are friendly and as eager as you to meet someone new.

- Talk to your RA. Resident advisors have had training in helping freshmen adjust to the new college environment. Alternately, visit the counselors at your school's counseling center. They have a lot of experience suggesting ways to get over homesickness.

- Stay in touch with your family and friends from home. E-mail a few photos through cyberspace to show off your new school. Regular phone calls home can be a lifeline as you settle into your college routine. And don't forget to write a good old-fashioned letter in which you share your experiences and impressions of your new environment.

- Consider getting involved in one of the many on-campus activities that excite you. This will keep you busy and will introduce you to new people.
- Resist running home at the first opportunity. Rather, start making plans for your visit home. Once you get over the hump of homesickness, you may very well be like one of my former students who recently told me after a summer of hard work after his freshman year, "I can't wait to go back."
- Pray. Praying will enhance your self-esteem. It will also reassure you of God's constant care for you, especially in your new surroundings.

Making Friends

"The better part of one's life consists of his friendships."
—ABRAHAM LINCOLN

Though you can remain loyal to your high-school friends through e-mail, phone calls, letters, and visits, forming new friendships is a sure-fire antidote to loneliness, homesickness, and yes, even "friend-sickness," during your freshman year. Developing new friendships can be a highlight of college life. Some of these new friends will remain so throughout your life. Many men and women have even met their future spouses in college.

Since your peer group is the most powerful influence on your personal growth in college, you need to have some friends as a network to survive the stresses and strains of undergraduate existence. But the good news is that it is not difficult to make friends in college because your classmates are also looking for friends. Another plus is that entering freshmen have a new lease on life. No one knows the reputation—good or bad—you might have had in high school. In fact, the freshman year is an opportune time to change one's image, especially if negative stereotypes have tarnished it.

For example, the high-school student who sloughed off studies or put down others can begin a college career with renewed enthusiasm, an energetic vigor for the intellectual life, and a wholesome openness to and appreciation for other people. He or she can abandon the dependence on preformed high-school cliques and the trivial high-school mind games to be the beautiful, unique, and good person he or she really is.

As you make new friends, first be careful not to latch on to your first campus acquaintance. Sometimes people lower their standards because they so desire any kind of relationship or they fear they won't find someone else. You have heard this advice before: *Be patient. Never do anything that makes you uncomfortable or that is wrong just to keep a friend.* Ben Franklin advised, "Be slow in choosing a friend, slower in changing." Here are some other pointers on making friends:

- **Make yourself available.** Expand beyond your high-school circle of friends. You are bound to find new friends if you try things like sitting in rows of classes with other students and not by yourself, joining others at a dining hall, studying in the library, leaving your dorm room door open, joining an on-campus activity, or participating in the social events sponsored by the orientation committee.

- **Be yourself.** Your honesty and sincerity will attract likewise authentic friends.

- **Be a good listener.** Dale Carnegie once wrote that you can make more friends in two months by getting interested in them than in two years trying to get them interested in you. Ask questions that focus on the other person: Where did you go to high school? What is your major? Why did you choose this college? How do you like the dining hall? Make eye contact with the person as he or she is speaking. Don't interrupt. Occasionally rephrase what the other person said. This shows you are interested and that you are indeed listening.

- **Smile.** It conveys warmth and good cheer. People like to be around those who are optimistic and happy.

- **Develop a closer relationship with Jesus.** Spend some time each day in prayer listening to the Lord. Share your concerns with him. If you imitate him by becoming a thoughtful, caring, sensitive individual, others will take note. Good people will want to be your friend.

- **Friendship requires commitment.** Realize that developing and maintaining a friendship requires time, energy, and love. Friendship involves both giving and receiving. Being there for a friend helps sustain and intensify your relationship. Therefore, be sure to factor time into your schedule to cultivate your friendships.

Dealing with Differences

"When you starts measuring somebody,
measure him right. . . .

Make sure you done taken into account what
hills and valleys he come through before he
got wherever he is."
—MAMA SPEAKING TO HER SON IN ACT 3 OF THE PLAY, *A RAISIN IN THE SUN*, BY LORRAINE HANSBERRY

One phenomenon you will notice immediately when arriving on a college campus is the great diversity among students. You will have classmates who are not only from a different place than you, but they will come from different religions and socioeconomic backgrounds than you. They will be a rainbow of races that trace their national identity to different countries and hold a host of political views. Some of your classmates will be homosexual. Others will have physical challenges. In addition, if you went to an all-boys or all-girls school, you will now have classmates of the opposite gender.

Most colleges draw students from every part of the country and from other nations around the world. These students have a myriad of interests and a smorgasbord of appealing talents. You will quickly notice more distinct clothing, hair styles (and colors), tattoos, and places for body piercing than you ever could have imagined. Some of your fellow students will flaunt their distinctiveness in order to underscore their desire to be individuals.

Today's universities actively support various diversity initiatives because research has shown that there are many positive benefits for students who live in our increasingly diverse society and interconnected world. Among other findings, a Ford Foundation study summarizing research on diversity on college campuses concludes that:

- Diversity initiatives have positive effects on both minority and majority students by improving their on-campus relationships. This results in more positive feelings about their campus involvement and their academic growth.
- Many students desire intergroup contact. When it happens it leads to increases in understanding and a lessening of prejudicial attitudes. It also positively affects academic success.

- Curricular diversity positively impacts "attitudes toward racial issues, on opportunities to interact in deeper ways with those who are different, and on overall satisfaction with the college or university. These benefits are particularly powerful for white students who have had less opportunity for such engagement."[9]

How should you react to diversity on your campus? First, remain calm! Meeting, interacting with, and learning from different people is a major goal of undergraduate education. We live in a pluralistic society where people from various backgrounds and widely varying views have agreed to live together in peace and harmony. This ideal social compact is, of course, sometimes tough to put into practice. The study cited above also reports that, despite diversity initiatives, many minority students still feel that the campus climate is unresponsive to their needs, past experiences, and educational expectations.[10] Colleges are not immune to the problems of the larger society. Racial tensions exist on college campuses. Homosexuals are targeted for violence and abuse. Vandalism occurs.

As you know, this illegal and immoral behavior is contrary to Jesus' law of love of neighbor. A life-giving truth our Lord revealed is that *all* people—no matter race, nationality, creed, or sexual orientation—are members of one human family. Thus, we are children of a compassionately loving God and brothers and sisters in Jesus Christ. Reacting to others not as aliens or enemies, but as real brothers and sisters, helps us accept and even appreciate God's plan of human diversity.

A person of faith knows that externals like skin color, language, musical tastes, political views, and the like, do not define what it means to be human. The essence of every human is invisible to the eye. Each person has incomparable worth and dignity.

One positive way to embrace the differences you experience is to look at them as learning opportunities. Meeting and getting to know different kinds of people can open you up to new ways of perceiving reality. More important, these people can become your friends.

Prejudice—judging someone on insufficient evidence—is the one barrier that can make it impossible to be open to those who are different. Prejudice is a learned behavior. It thrives on stereotyping, that is, judging a person or a whole group of people by exaggerating one trait or quality. It manifests itself in un-Christian behavior like verbal abuse (e.g., telling racist jokes), avoidance, discrimination, physical violence, and even killing. Prejudice, however, can be overcome. It can be unlearned through exposure with an open mind to different people and then to accepting them as individuals.

Do you need to accept everything about a person who is different? No. Obviously, some qualities a person has no control over—gender, race, nationality, the region from which he or she comes. To reject a person because of these externals is narrow-minded, wrong, and even sinful. But people do have control over their *behavior*. For example, you can accept and must love a person who has a homosexual orientation. Most people do not choose this condition. But you don't have to buy into the secular philosophy that homosexual *behavior* is moral and a licit option for human relationships. Being open-minded is not equivalent to "everything goes." Christians are called to love all people. However, Christians do not have to accept behaviors or political views or practices that are destructive, harmful, and sinful.

A final comment: This section of the chapter encourages love and respect for people who differ from you. It is an unfortunate reality, though, that you may not find the same degree of acceptance of yourself or your views at your college. For example, if you are pro-life, an advocate of traditional values, and a supporter of orthodox Catholic moral teaching, you may find your views ridiculed, especially in many of your classes. You may also find it more difficult to find an openness to positions that do not fit the current "political correctness" enforcers of the day. Many of my students, including my own children, have found this to be the case. Your open acceptance of others as persons may not translate into others accepting you because of your religious views. In other words, you may be on the receiving end of ridicule simply because you are a believing and practicing Christian.

Joining Up

*"Any activity becomes creative when
the doer cares about doing it right or better."*
—JOHN UPDIKE

Shortly after you arrive on campus—perhaps as part of your orientation—the myriad activities available to you as an undergraduate will vie for your attention. Should you join a club or participate in an activity? If so, how many? These two questions will demand an answer in your first month at college.

Think of all the extracurricular offerings as part of a buffet table. The trouble with eating from a buffet line is the tendency to overindulge. A glut of extracurricular activities is not something you need your first semester of college. Always keep in mind that your top priority is academics. Everything else is secondary.

Consider signing up for just *one* activity your first semester. As noted earlier, joining a club or engaging in an activity can help you feel connected to your college community and alleviate some of the symptoms of homesickness. In choosing an activity, these are the types of questions you can ask yourself:

- Will being in this club make my life more enjoyable? Will it be fun?
- How will this activity help me grow as a person? Will it help me develop my talents?
- What benefit does this club have for my future, especially my career or vocation? The popular book by Patrick Combs, *Major in Success*, has as one of its theses that you should engage in activities in college that will help you get your dream job after college.[11] Employers look to your college involvement (work experience, internships, co-ops, extracurricular activities) as an important factor in whether you will be a successful employee. It is not a bad idea to begin thinking of your résumé even as early as your first semester. Just don't overdo it.

When choosing an activity, seriously consider one that is service-oriented. Serving others helps you take your mind off yourself and your own problems. For example, what really helped me my first semester away from home was getting up every Sunday morning to teach catechism classes at an inner-city parish in Chicago. The discipline of serving youngsters helped me overcome homesickness. I was in control of something; at the same time, it made me feel good about myself in my new surroundings. I was doing good for others. A wise person summarized it well: "Service is the price we pay for the space we occupy."

If you decide to engage in an activity your first semester, be faithful to the time commitment it requires. People will depend on you.

This is another reason not to overindulge in extracurricular activities until you know what you can handle. After your first-semester grades come in, reassess your extracurricular involvement. Adjust your commitments accordingly.

Having started this chapter with Robert Fulghum, take some time to analyze the rules that he, and probably, you learned in kindergarten. These are valuable even for college freshmen:[12]

1. Play fair.
2. Don't hit people.
3. Put things back where you found them.
4. Clean up your own mess.
5. Don't take things that aren't yours.
6. Say you're sorry when you hurt somebody.
7. Wash your hands before you eat.
8. Take a nap everyday.
9. Flush.

THINK ABOUT IT

- Know who will be there when you need help.
- If you plan to fail, you are planning to fail.
- *Japanese proverb*: "Fall seven times, stand up eight."
- If you want others to respect you, you must respect yourself.

Hitting the Books

3

A diligent freshman went to her first English literature class and sat in the front row. The professor immediately told the class that they would be reading five books during the term, and that he would be giving them a list of authors from which to choose. Then, he went to the lectern, opened his class book, and rattled off some names: "Abbott, Bruce, Carey, Carson, Dooley. . . . "

The conscientious freshman feverishly began to scribble down the names in her notebook. Moments later, she felt a tap on her shoulder from the guy sitting behind her. "Don't jot notes. He's only taking attendance." [1]

The freshman described above may have been a bit overzealous, but she certainly realized that a key to academic success is the taking of good class notes. This chapter will treat some topics of vital interest for college success, including:

- Choosing a major
- Time management
- Going to class
- Study tips
- Test-taking
- Writing papers

Choosing a Major

"One should be able to distinguish between
good, bad, and downright awful."
—ISAIAH BERLIN

The most popular major for college freshmen is "undecided." Almost three out of four incoming college freshmen do not know what to choose for a major.[2] Should this be a source of concern at this stage of your career? No. The president of a Jesuit university told me that the average undergraduate changes majors three times during college. Even if you have already "decided" on one major, this does not guarantee that you will graduate with the same one.

Put your choice of a college major in perspective. The more fundamental question to consider about your college education is this: *Are you here to prepare for a living or to prepare for life?* The issue is not really what you are going to *do* with your life. The central question is what are you going to *be*. What kind of person do you wish to become?

The rush to choose a major is often a symptom of society's desire to have you fit into the system. This system lionizes material wealth, unthinking consumerism, and blind acceptance of the superficial status quo.

An educated Christian will at least pause and ask: "Why am I *really* majoring in this subject? Is it merely a stepping stone to an easy life? Or is it a means to a good life—a life of serving other people?"

Take some time to wrestle with these foundational questions because they are more important for your ultimate happiness than your choice of a major. Meanwhile, concentrate on taking courses in the core subjects, for example, English, a foreign language, and math or science. Resolve to do well in these courses. Leave room for an additional elective or two to help you experience what might later become a major course of study.

If possible, sign up for an outstanding professor who excites students about the subject matter. (Consult with a couple of serious-minded juniors or seniors. They'll be glad to level with you.) The course title is not important for profs like this. Their joyful presentation of their field may very well be the catalyst that will turn you on to a new course of study that you never considered before.

Here are three other steps that can help you choose a major.

1. Seek God's plan for your life.

The key to both happiness and holiness is doing God's will. How often we pray "Thy will be done" in the Lord's Prayer, yet make our own plans and then petition God to support them? This is doing things backwards and can really lead to unhappiness and confusion. Being "in sync" with God's plans is a much surer path to peace and happiness.

Your most basic decision starting out in college is not choosing a major but choosing to follow God's plan for your life. If you say "yes" to following God's will, then he will send you grace-filled insights to lead you in one direction rather than another. For your part, you must pay attention to the details in your life and how God is working in it. Spend time discerning God's will for you by asking yourself:

- What are your deepest inclinations? What subjects and topics really engage you? What do you really enjoy? Note how your mind, body, emotions, and spirit react to various subjects. Don't be afraid to trust your deepest intuitions. Ordinarily, God works through these attractions and probably implanted them in you in the first place.

- When more than one possible choice confronts you, which—in your imagination—brings you the most peace? Which seems the more natural "fit" for your personality and talents? If you are truly doing God's will, you will experience a profound sense that what you decided is right.

2. Reflect on your interests.

Part of what college is all about is to continue to discover your talents and to think about different ways you can use them to serve others and to make a relatively happy life for yourself.

Many students choose majors based on their gut-level reaction to certain subjects they've taken in school in the past. These reactions are often a good guide, especially if they correspond to a real love for a particular subject matter. Other students choose majors based on psychological testing of their interests, for example, by taking an interest-inventory in high-school or reading a book on vocational choices. Both of these approaches have merit and can help you determine a major. For example:

- *Are you an idea person?* Do thinking, reading, talking, and writing about ideas turn you on? Do you like solving problems? Are you good at communicating your thoughts? Do you like debating themes in movies, editorials, books you read? If so, then maybe philosophy, English, or the sciences might be a good major for you.

- *Are you a people person?* Do you like learning why people and societies act the way they do? Are you outgoing? Do you love to talk to and associate with people? Do you empathize with others, putting yourself in their place and looking at issues from their point of view? Do you want to deal with lots of people on a daily basis? If so, maybe you should think about teaching, nursing, psychology, sociology, or one of the performing arts.

- *Do you like to tinker with things?* Are you a computer whiz? Do you like taking things apart and putting them back together? Do you like to express your intelligence through things you've made or discovered? Are you curious about how the natural world operates? If so, the physical and natural sciences, engineering, experimental psychology, or various arts may be for you.

One of the most highly regarded categorizations of determining what career might be good for you, based on your interests and abilities, comes from the studies of Dr. John Holland.[3] Sample assessments based on his work can be found on the Internet. His categories seek to discover if you are:

- **Realistic** (practical, outdoors person, mechanically inclined, athletic, etc.). If so, majors to consider would be those in the technical field, engineering, and agriculture.

- **Investigative** (analytical, precise, independent worker, abstract thinker, etc.). Possible majors for this type of person are math, science, and philosophy.

- **Artistic** (creative, imaginative, individualistic, etc.). Suitable majors would include music, literature, and drama.

- **Social** (idealistic, helpful, outgoing, etc.). You may wish to consider nursing, teaching, communications, and social work.

- **Enterprising** (assertive, persuasive, energetic, etc.). Potential majors for this type of person would be business, marketing, and pre-law.

- **Conventional** (accurate, methodical, efficient, structured, etc.).
  Business, accounting, and computer science are among some
  compatible majors.

Chances are that two or three of these categories describe you,
thus giving you several majors that may match your interests.
Remember that your freshman year is a good time to monitor what
attracts you. Explore many interests. There is no barrier to a career for
a person who loves learning. College is a time to develop your talents
and learn your likes and dislikes. There will be plenty of time in later
years to think about how you can translate your major into a job. Now
is the time when you should throw yourself into college life and enjoy
the many opportunities.

Also know that a college major is not your ultimate decision in
life. An interesting fact is that while your college major has some
direct bearing on your first job after graduation, labor experts predict
that you will change careers as many as five times as you move
through the twenty-first century. Many professionals and happy, well-
adjusted people are working in fields totally unrelated to their college
majors. For example, I have had students who majored in English and
are now surgeons, or majored in music and are now successful entre-
preneurs, or majored in business and are teaching English. It is true,
however, that for many there is a close relationship between their college major and their careers. There are likely more medical doctors
who majored in biology or chemistry than history.

Think of your college degree as a credential that can help put you
on a career path. It cannot *guarantee* that you will be a psychologist or
a lawyer or an accountant. For many careers, you will need advanced
education in graduate or professional school or as an intern on the job.

In general, it is good advice to major in what interests you the
most and what really turns you on. You might even consider a double
major, especially if you are coming into college with some Advanced-
Placement credit. Then, simply trust that there will be many careers to
match your interests.

A reality check involves your ability. For example, your performance in certain courses can limit your choices for a college major.
Many freshmen begin the year majoring in biology or chemistry with
the intention of becoming doctors. But a below-average grade or

extreme difficulty in the required course convinces them the major (and career) wasn't for them. Use your own capacity to handle a certain subject academically, emotionally, and physically to help you choose a major.

3. Begin some career exploration.

You can also work in reverse in selecting your major if you have definite ideas about your interest in a career. You can check the following resources to help you to make a decision:

- Your **college's course catalog,** for information about courses that might interest you and requirements for a major.
- Other **students**, especially seniors, to see how they chose a major, whether or not they are happy with their choices, and various requirements for their fields of study.
- Your **college's career center**, an underutilized resource, for information on summer jobs, internships, how and when to choose a major. Make it a top priority to visit this center during your first semester.
- Your **professors** and **academic advisor,** for ideas about your potential major. Many of them have practical, "real-world" experience in your areas of interest.
- The **Internet,** which has lots of information on careers, labor statistics, and job trends.
- **Alumni, family, friends**, especially if they have a job that you would love to have someday. What was their college major? How did they get into their field?

Planning: Time Management

> *"There are thinkers and there are doers.*
> *Then there are those who think a lot about doing."*
> —ANONYMOUS

At least four types of freshmen roam the campus. *Drifters* have no sense of direction. They lack self-discipline and are easily distracted and led by others. *Dreamers* are subject to wishful and usually unrealistic thinking. They are controlled by a "shoulda, coulda, woulda" mentality. *Demons* are hell-bent on having fun. They tend to be angry, competitive, discontented, and restless blamers. Finally, there are the *Doers* who are self-directed and organized. They set realistic priorities, make and keep schedules, and assume responsibility.

Drifters rarely make it to sophomore year. Dreamers may survive first semester, but only if they shake themselves from their sleep walk and get organized. Demons may make it but they are never happy, and college is a joyless burden. Doers succeed. They pay the price for success, but to them the gain is worth the pain. They have a plan, and they sacrifice to stick to it. Invariably, they get good, if not excellent, grades.

A major part of a Doer's success is effective *time management*. Perhaps the biggest element of your success freshman year is your realistic grasp of several essential truths:

- There is never enough time to do all that needs to be done.
- Everything takes longer than you think it is going to take.
- Human nature is tempted to procrastinate. (The American humorist Don Marquis defined procrastination as "the art of keeping up with yesterday.")

You can learn to deal with these truths if you decide right *now* to do what it takes to manage your time well. The benefits are many because effective time management helps you:

- Set priorities for the day, week, month, and semester ahead
- avoid conflicts and unplanned events
- evaluate your progress for test preparation, project completion, and paper writing
- take advantage of opportunities (e.g., knowing when to use limited resources like books on the library reserve shelf)
- dodge those anxious "I'm-always-behind-and-don't-know-where-I'm-going" feelings
- study smarter, not harder
- avoid both stress and guilt by staying on schedule, thus allowing you to feel good about yourself and more relaxed during times you reserve for fun
- be in control.

Drifters and dreamers typically think that college's main purpose is fun. If this is their top priority, then only rarely will they attain academic success. In contrast, doers look on studying as their main responsibility. For them, college is like a job with a 45-hour work week. This is a realistic goal given the 168 hours in a week. Here's how a basic time management plan might break down:

classes	15
studying	30
church	1
sleep	56 (8 hours per night)
socializing/eating	21 (3 hours per day)
free time	45 (equivalent of another work week!)
Total	168

One of the advantages of living in a dorm is that you won't waste time commuting to school. You are already there, but you will still have to plan to get to class on time. As a college student, you will be in class only three or four hours a day. In fact, some days you might not even have a class. Compare this to your eight-hour high-school day. Also, you have a seven-day period, not five, to stretch out your 30 hours of studying.

Here's one way of looking at it: If you would study five hours each day Monday through Thursday, and sneak in two hours of study between Friday's classes, you would only have eight hours of study to do Saturday and Sunday. You could take every Friday night off and decide how *you* want to spend your weekends.

The National Study of Student Engagement conducted by Indiana University revealed how most first-year students at four-year liberal arts colleges fall way short of the recommended two hours of preparation for each class attended.[4] (This would average 30 hours of study for a student carrying a 15-hour course load, the full-time job mindset.) Class preparation was defined as "studying, reading, writing, rehearsing, and other activities." Here are the national averages for freshmen:

HOURS SPENT PREPARING FOR CLASS	PERCENT FOR FIRST-YEAR STUDENTS
1–5 hours	18
6–10 hours	24
11–15 hours	20
16–20 hours	16
21–25 hours	10
26–30 hours	6
30+ hours	5

Imagine how well *you* will do if you stick to a realistic work schedule as outlined here. You will be in the elite five percent of students who are serious about their studies. You are bound to do well. You will also benefit from another big payoff to this suggested time control: Fun without guilt! Social pleasure without sacrificing good grades.

Organize your time according to these three principles, and you are bound to succeed:

1. Work for an A in every course during your first semester.

Most of your classmates won't do this, so you will stand out. By committing yourself to this goal first semester, you'll know what it takes to get high grades. You may decide later that it is not worth putting in the kind of time necessary to get a 3.8, for example. Nevertheless, you'll never know what is needed for this level of accomplishment unless you commit yourself to this goal early in your career. Even if you don't attain your goal, your disciplined work habits will get you off to an excellent start. Many of my former students have taken this advice and told me that it gave them the psychological boost that gave them the confidence that they could indeed thrive in college.

2. Create a homework schedule and always stick to it.

Remember the image of college as a job. If you fail to show up for work, your boss will dock your pay, overlook you at promotion time, and eventually fire you. Cut out study time and you'll eventually pay for it severely. You may remember this experience as a high-school student: you regretted not spending an extra few minutes studying for an exam when you eventually missed a higher grade by only one or two percentage points. Just like staying on task at a paid job, sticking to your homework schedule means committing yourself:

- to say "no" to your friends who want to party when it conflicts with your schedule;
- to not watch television, play computer games, or surf the Internet until you are finished with the tasks at hand.

3. Work ahead of schedule.

It's likely that, in a given week, especially at the start of the semester, you won't have thirty hours of homework. Great! Use these bonus hours to work ahead. You have no idea how being ahead in every class will help you relax. It is true in college that if you don't keep ahead of your schedule then in reality you are behind. If you aim simply to stay on schedule, then any unforeseen emergency or sickness or surprise visit from a high-school friend will make you fall behind. If this happens when a major assignment or test is due, it may cause serious academic stumbling.

To stay ahead of the pack, why not begin working on that paper that your professor assigned the very first day of class? Use the light schedule in the early weeks to do preliminary research and writing. Or read ahead in the assigned texts. Doing so will help you profit much more from a prof's lecture.

CALENDARS AND CHARTS

Time management is a matter of organization. Obtain and use the following to help you get and remain organized through each term:

- **Large wall calendar.** The very first day that you receive them, carefully review the course syllabi your professors give you in each of your courses. (Often these can be obtained online.) Immediately list on a large wall calendar the deadlines for tests, lab reports, term papers, and major homework assignments. Use a different ink color for each subject. Note common due dates and begin immediately to map out strategies for completing the glut of the work. *Suggestion:* Create your own *earlier* deadlines for big projects like term papers.

- **Flow chart/project board.** This is especially helpful for the systematic planning of term papers. List your own deadlines for completing topic selection, initial Web and library research, preliminary outline, further Web and library research, revised outline, rough draft, proofing by self and another, and final draft. Finish a week early to avoid panic attacks and to create cushion time for emergencies. Pulling "all-nighters" rarely results in your best work.

- **Monthly desk calendar.** Transcribe the data from the wall calendar onto your desk calendar. Add homework assignments and other obligations that you'll have during the month.

- **Pocket daily organizer with hour-by-hour listings (alternative preferred by some: PDA [Personal Digital Assistant]).** Fill each hour for the coming week on Sunday night and revise as needed during the week. Follow this plan:
  - Make a "to-do" list, ranking high- to low-priority obligations. Cross off items as you accomplish them. This will give you a psychological boost, a feeling of progress.
  - Include fixed times like classes, meals, errands, meetings, exercise, and prayer, as well as time for socializing. But be sure to factor in four to five hours of good study time per day, Monday through Thursday. This will help you go a long way toward meeting the suggested 30 hours per week of study time. Plan your weekend to suit your social life, but also allow for about eight hours of study.

- Schedule your study times for when you function best. A good rule of thumb: Schedule top "to-dos" when you have peak energy. Studies have shown that humans are more alert when the sun is up. If this is true for you, then study your toughest subject during the daylight hours.
- Be specific. For example, in your 7–8:30 p.m. slot, instead of writing "study psychology," note "read psych text, Chapter 5."
- Stick to your study time in the schedule. Remember it is your top priority. Use your schedule as an excuse to break off from things that eat up time, including conversations with friends.
- Look at your daily calendar every day, first thing in the morning. This will help you plan your day efficiently. For example, take what you need for a trip to the library between your first two classes along with your class supplies. This will save you wasted steps and time going back to retrieve them from your dorm room or car.

In the Classroom

"It is easier to keep up than to catch up."
—AN "A" STUDENT

College classes are organized and scheduled much differently than high-school classes. Some introductory lecture classes are in large halls with more than one hundred students; other small seminar groups have as few as three or four students. Compared to high school, college classes meet less frequently, at most three times a week. Some evening courses assemble only once a week. College courses typically require long-term projects, with little daily homework. Don't be surprised if a given course only has three assessments: a midterm, a comprehensive final, and a major paper or project.

The self-discipline needed for success in college begins with going to class. Many professors don't take attendance. There is no dean of students to hassle you about not coming to class. However, other professors enforce a strict attendance policy like the following:

"Attendance is required. Missing more than one class is hazardous to your grade; missing more than two WILL result in a lower grade."

College equals personal responsibility. You have to be in charge of your education from being present in class (yes, even at 8:00 a.m. if you signed up for an early class) through studying, writing papers, working on individual or group projects, and passing exams. Remember this important lesson: Academic success begins by being present. Here are some keys to get off to a good start:

Attend class! Regular class attendance is vital for good grades. You can't expect to rely on the note-taking of a friend to get you through. Rather, make a point to be present at the beginning of the session for important review. Stay to the end of the class period when quizzes and assignments are sometimes given. By now you have discovered that all grading has a subjective element to it. Regular class attendance *does* influence many professors to perceive you in a positive light. Profs often give the benefit of the doubt to those who show an interest in their courses.

Give your profs the chance to get to know you by face and name. Sitting front and center has four major benefits:
- It will enable you to make eye contact with the teacher. (Profs are human. They like an audience. They'll notice and appreciate your positive feedback.)
- It will help you avoid distractions, like daydreaming and looking out the window.
- It will position you well to see visual materials, like Powerpoint™ presentations.
- It will facilitate more direct access with both your professor and classmates when you want to ask questions or contribute your observations.

By the way, don't hesitate to participate by asking questions. I had a course with one of the most highly regarded scholars in his field. He treated each question—no matter how simplistic—with great respect. He even thanked the questioner for raising the point. The only dumb question is the unasked one. Questions show you are interested, and they help clarify information for you and your classmates.

Attendance on the first day of the term is especially important. Make sure you understand the items on the syllabus, your road map for the course. If your prof fails to provide it in class, ask if it can be downloaded from his Web site. Be sure to know exactly what elements will go into your grade. How many tests will there be? Does the course require a paper or some other project? Will the final exam be comprehensive? Do homework assignments factor into the grade? Will the prof give extra credit? These are all-important questions that should be answered on the first day.

Come to class prepared. Make sure you read the text ahead of time. Note the important points from the chapter. Being able to identify them will help you know what key points will likely come up in the day's lecture. Arrive to class at least five minutes early and sit front and center, especially in a large lecture hall. Take a few minutes to review your notes from the previous class to help you transition into the upcoming class. Have your writing materials ready. By being a bit ahead of schedule you are in a much better position for academic success.

Take good notes. Use a separate 8 1/2" x 11" size notebook for each course. I also recommend a binder-type notebook so you can easily insert notes and class handouts in the appropriate places. Write your name, address, and phone number in it in case of loss. Date your notes for each day you are in class. Get the phone number and e-mail address of a classmate and keep them in a safe place. You'll never know when you'll need a lifesaver if you happen to lose your notebook before a test. Or you may wish to get together with classmates to study now and then.

Write your notes legibly; you simply won't have the time to go back and rewrite them. Take notes in outline form to help you see the flow of the presentations as developed by the lecturer. Write on only the right 3/4 of the page. Use the left 1/4 of the page for your own questions, notes, and thoughts. When it comes time to review the notes, you might find it helpful to cover the right side of the page and try to recall the main points from the cue words you have written in your space on the left.

Use a good-flowing pen to help you write quickly. Always keep a backup pen on hand. Highlight key terms and definitions so they stand out when you review your notes.

If the professor asks questions to engage students in the lecture, volunteer to answer ones that you know. One advantage is that you will be less likely to be called on to recite for ones that you don't know, saving yourself from some potential embarrassment.

Pay close attention to the various hints that profs give to underscore what is important and notable. Copy into your notebook *everything* they write on the board. Pay close attention to any diagrams they put on the overhead. Watch their nonverbal communication for points of emphasis. Note anything they repeat. Be on the lookout for buzz words like, "This is important," "I can't stress enough . . .," "The third key reason is. . . ." Profs also cue test questions: "Is this clear?" "Anyone who doesn't understand this?" When they ask for your close attention, give it to them with a pen in hand.

For daily note-taking, try to understand what the prof is saying. Put the lecture into your own words by summarizing the main ideas and giving examples. Use abbreviations to speed up your writing, but resist copying *everything* the prof says. Always note definitions and jot down lists or enumerated points. Besides underlining or highlighting key points, use asterisks, exclamation points, question marks. Draw arrows.

Review class lectures as soon as possible. Some studies claim that you will lose more than 50 percent of processed information within an hour of departing from the classroom. And you will lose up to 75 percent within a day! Therefore, a great way to prepare for your tests is to review the course lecture right after class. Superior students review class notes daily. Go back over the lecture with a highlighter to emphasize key points. Then compress these highlights to a few key points that will help you remember the major ideas.

Repetition is the key to memory. Studies have also shown that most people need to review material seven times to get it into their memories. The most productive review time is right after class.

Seek help if you are confused. If you don't understand something, or are struggling in a course, get help. In large lecture classes, befriend the TA (teaching assistant). Be cordial with department secretaries if you must go through them to get an appointment with your professor. Most professors note their office hours in the syllabus or post them on their Web site. Simply by visiting the prof you give a strong indication that you care about the course and that you are trying. When you go to get help, be prepared to ask specific questions concerning your trouble spots.

If tutoring is offered at your college, use the service, by all means. Join a study group or form one with a couple of other classmates. Visit the learning center to get help on how to take notes and read more productively. If you are struggling in a Composition 101 class, go to the writing center once a week. It is a sign of strength, not weakness, to know when to ask for help.

Study Tips

> *"There are no secrets to success. It is the result of preparation, hard work, and learning from failure."*
> —COLIN POWELL

Success in college is directly proportional to productive study sessions. A comfortable study area and consistent study time are essential preconditions for two necessary study skills: fruitful text reading and memorizing information to master tests.

The Study Area

How lucky for you if your dorm room is quiet enough for you to study in it. If not, then stake a claim to a table in a dorm study room, a carrel in the library, or a desk in an empty classroom, providing it is a designated and safe area for study. Wherever you end up studying regularly, you will want to make it accessible, convenient, and pleasant. Basics include a comfortable chair, decent lighting, good ventilation, and a cool temperature (if it is too hot, you'll fall asleep). Many people like to study with music in the background because it serves as "white noise" that camouflages other distracting sounds. Familiar instrumental music with steady rhythms is less distracting than music with lyrics, a variety of rhythms, and high decibels.

Distractions are the curse of serious students. Reduce external distractions by turning off your cell phone and avoiding the television. If you find your study sessions unproductive, try changing the environment. It may be as simple as rearranging the top of your desk or finding an alternative study area. It is a good idea to have a backup place for those times when a study session is not going well because of one distraction or another. A change of scenery can help you refocus and settle down. This is especially true if you get the strong urge to nap, or are battling daydreaming or boredom. Better to go to the library than be tempted to lie on the bed. Counteract other internal distractions like hunger by eating a light snack before studying.

What Time Is Best for Study?

Everyone has a peak study time for doing the most productive studying, a block of time in the morning or in the evening. Determine when you study best and make this time sacrosanct. Reserve up to four consecutive hours. Stick to this study time, even if you don't feel like studying. The discipline of keeping a regular schedule will turn you into a true student. It will give you an edge over those who decide to study just when they "feel" like it.

Make a prioritized "study list." Work on your most difficult, least favorite, or high-priority assignments first during your peak energy time. Allot enough time to finish this difficult task before moving on to another. Don't rush through one assignment just to get to another. But do cross off items on your list once you finish them. It will give you a good feeling of accomplishment and a renewed sense of purpose to continue.

You will find your study sessions more enjoyable and productive if you study dissimilar subject areas back-to-back. For example, work some math problems after reading a history chapter. By the way, it is usually less fatiguing to do text reading *before* doing interactive work like math problems.

Reward good study habits with frequent breaks, say ten minutes for each 50 minutes of study. (But avoid watching television during a break or you might get hooked on a program that will torpedo your good resolve.) After a tough week of study (e.g., for a midterm or final), add a special reward like going out for dinner, taking in a movie, or making two or three phone calls to old friends. Be sure to break up your study times with exercise. Exercise relieves tension and makes you think more clearly.

Don't limit your study time simply to the scheduled peak energy period. Capture a spare half-hour here or there between classes to do text reading. One estimate claims that college students average ten pages of reading per day in each class. These seventy pages per week per course of varying degrees of difficulty can seem overwhelming. Yet, it is amazing how you can whittle this task down to size by using those spare "empty times" that appear in every college student's schedule.

Finally, be sure to leave enough study time for tests. Your best preparation for exams is to review your class notes faithfully and intelligently each day. Your next best practice for test preparation is to do a brief review of each course each week. Allow at least two nights to study for a regular exam, approximately six hours on average. Break this period into smaller chunks of time. Six one-half hour sessions are a lot more productive than one marathon all-nighter.

How to Read a Text

A large percentage of your typical college homework assignments consists of reading textbooks and journal articles given as handouts or which you will download off the Internet. But reading from texts and scholarly articles differs from reading an enjoyable novel. You will have to prove that you actually understand what you read, usually by passing an exam. The following "SQ4R method" characterizes a good approach to reading.[5] Here are its steps:

- **S=Survey.** A good start to a text-reading assignment is quickly to survey the chapter or assignment. Begin by reading any summary points or the questions at the end of the assignment to see what you should focus on. Read the introduction to get an overview of the material. Note any text set off by bullets or boldface as well as charts and illustrations. Five or ten minutes spent surveying the material may be the best time you spend on your assignment.

- **Q=Question.** Look at the heading of each text section. Formulate the heading as a who, what, where, why, or how question that you want the section to answer. For example, "Blood Vessels: The Roadways of the Body" becomes "Why are blood vessels known as the roadway of the body?" Try to guess what a test question based on this section might look like.

- **R1=Read.** Read at a good clip so you don't get bogged down in minute details. Read for understanding the big picture. After you've read through the material once, go back over a section and use a *bright* yellow highlighter to mark terms, definitions, and key points. (Avoid underlining with a ruler since it is too mechanical and time-consuming.) Highlight no more than a third of the material or you'll defeat the purpose of highlighting: to extract essential information only. Draw arrows, stars, or lines in the margins to call attention to important examples or key points. Place a question mark next to a paragraph that confuses you or which you want to ask about in class. Then do make it a point to ask about this material in class.

- **R2=Recite.** After reading a few pages, look up and recite aloud the answers to the questions you formulated in the question step. Put the author's main points into your own words. If you go blank, read through the material again. If you don't get it now, you won't get it on the test. Don't rush this step.

- **R3=Record.** Jot key points from your highlighted material into your notebook. Condense the main ideas into your own words. Review the questions you formulated from the headings and subheadings: the "Who? What? How? Why?" Note only the essential information.

- **R4=Review.** Stop periodically to look over your highlighted material and your notes. Concentrate on learning and remembering these points. You might once again want to engage your senses by reciting the key points aloud. Also, answer any study questions provided in the chapter. The review questions are intended to see whether you grasp the main concepts. Besides, profs like to re-form study questions and use them on tests.

When you start using this method, you'll find that it might take a little longer than what you are used to (one estimate is ten to fifteen percent longer than a traditional approach). But the payoff is huge. Research has shown that using this method of surveying, questioning the material, and then reading for understanding, reciting, recording, and reviewing results in a 70 percent increase in retention after two months of using it. The payoff: considerably less time studying for tests.

Memorizing Material for Tests

Before you begin to memorize for a test, make sure it is correct. Check and match your class and text notes with study guide information and text summaries. Then create your own study guide. Begin by rereading your notes and highlighted materials. Distill this information down to its essentials and type it out to create your own personal test study guide.

Next, organize your time for fruitful study sessions. Periodic sessions of 15 to 20 minutes in duration are more productive than two-hour sessions of straight memorizing. A good time to memorize is right before going to sleep. Follow up with a review immediately after waking up.

It helps to know what type of learning style you have to help you memorize and effectively involve your senses. For example, if you are a *visual* learner (about 65 percent of the population is), you study best when the material is graphic. You will find studying alone in a quiet place most effective. Whenever possible, be sure to write down your words and use graphs, tables, and drawings to help you memorize information. *Auditory* learners (30 percent of the population) like to hear the material. Reading aloud and talking to themselves are effective for them to get the material into their memory banks. *Kinesthetic* learners (5 percent) learn best when they touch and are physically involved in their learning. They like to move around; background noise actually helps them focus. If you learn best this way, make your study sessions more physical by pacing, standing at a desk, using colored markers, changing the environment, and visualizing the task at hand. A *mixed-modality* learner (most people) can and does learn using all three of the styles.

Involving your senses can help all learning styles. Look at your notes (sight), rewrite your notes by condensing (touch), and say your notes aloud (hearing). All of these techniques helped me to memorize material. First, I would condense all my notes to a page or two. Then I'd read them repeatedly, making sure that I really understood the concepts. (Understanding makes memorizing easier and is the purpose of learning.) Finally, I'd take a walk, saying the notes aloud until I had them memorized. I'd test my retention by speaking the notes aloud until I was confident that I knew them.

Other helpful hints for improving your memory:
- *Maintain a healthy lifestyle.* If you drink alcohol, do so in moderation. Studies have shown that consuming two or three drinks on four different days per week inhibits cognitive ability, including memory. Smoking constricts blood vessels in the brain. Exhaustion caused by too little sleep interferes with forming new memories and retaining them. A healthy diet, vigorous exercise, managing stress, and getting enough sleep all help you retain information.

- *Overlearn the material.* Even after you think you have mastered the material, try to pose new questions to yourself. Repeat and rehearse until you get it down perfectly.
- *Study similar material on different days.* Trying to remember material that is very similar can lead to interference. For example, you will remember the list of bones in the hand and another list of bones in the feet better if you learn them on different days.
- *Write out and organize your information.* Merely writing something down helps you learn. Organizing lists or making comparison/contrast charts can help sink information into your memory.
- *Create mnemonic devices like acronyms and acrostics.* Acronyms are words made from the first letters of other words. I still remember one I learned in high school that describes Wordsworth's nineteenth century concept of the Romantic spirit: *SOOPERIT* ("spontaneous overflow of powerful emotion recollected in tranquillity"). These don't have to be real words. Acrostics are invented sentences. Perhaps you learned this famous example to help remember the order of notes on sheet music—EGBDF—"Every Good Boy Does Fine." Similarly, create outlandish images to help you with vocabulary words and definitions. This can be especially helpful in learning a foreign language.
- *Use different colored highlight markers for your review notes.* Creative page layout is an effective way to better envision your notes.
- *Cluster information.* Group apparent isolated facts, numbers, and letters into manageable "chunks." It is tough to memorize 275837466; it is easier to remember 275 837 466.
- *Avoid cramming.* Hasty and intense preparation for tests known as cramming heightens anxiety and is not conducive to retaining information.

Study Groups and Seeking Help

Some students derive great benefit by participating in study groups with other students. Others find them a big waste of time, especially if members come unprepared or are not serious. Study groups should never substitute for doing your own homework, text reading, or problem-solving.

An ideal size for a study group is four to six members. Strive to find members who will pull their own weight, ones who will be as talented, serious-minded, and hardworking as you, if not more so. Good study groups meet at the same time and place each week and set an agenda ahead of time. For example, they compose and answer possible test questions, drill essential material, and create anagrams to help remember key concepts.

Be sure to look into a study group sponsored by the course's prof or grad assistants. These groups often walk you through some practice exams and help you focus on skills needed to pass an upcoming test.

Also, don't be ashamed or shy if you are struggling in a course. Get help *before* you fail! If early intervention does not help you improve your grade, you should have time to drop the course. (Check your college catalogue for the final acceptable date to drop courses without a penalty). Make an appointment with your professor; most are eager to help struggling students. Follow their recommendations: join a study group, seek a tutor, go to the campus academic services center. The campus life office or student affairs center will suggest many resources at your college to help you get through a tough course.

Test-Taking Tips

"I was thrown out of college for cheating on the metaphysics exam; I looked into the soul of the boy sitting next to me."
—WOODY ALLEN

Here's a quick thought: the average college student takes about 130 exams from freshman year to graduation. You can't get through college without passing more than a few tests! A good test assesses student learning in a challenging, yet fair, way. Tests are time-honored methods to get feedback on the effectiveness of the teaching-learning process. This section lists some ways to survive college tests.

Preparation

One good way to prepare for tests is to ace any routine quizzes the prof gives. These not only boost your grade but can give you an idea of what kind of information will be on the midterm or final. Be sure to keep these quizzes and study from them in preparation for your larger exams.

Also, pay close attention in class for any hints the professor might give during his daily lectures. For example, she might ask rhetorically "Wouldn't this make a great test question?" Note the question in your notebook and be sure to prepare an answer for it. It may well appear on the exam.

On a weekly basis, review your class and text notes trying to discover what you don't know. Check with other students to fill in gaps in your notes. Then, two or three days before the test, begin your review by condensing your notes, creating anagrams, making flash cards, and constructing outlines and diagrams. Verbalize the review material.

An excellent preparation technique is to anticipate test questions and practice answering them. Study groups can be especially helpful in creating these practice questions. If at all possible, see if you can obtain copies of "retired tests" to see what kinds of questions your professor might ask. Some past tests may be on file in the library. You can get others from fraternity files, students who took the course before, or teaching assistants.

Prepare especially well for the first test in a course. Don't be afraid to over-study. An excellent grade on the first test will get you off to a good start and help you "bank" points for later exams.

Get a good night's sleep before a test. Come to class dressed comfortably. For a longer testing period, bring a high-protein snack and a drink. Also, bring a watch to help you keep up a good pace during the exam.

When You Are Given the Test

Read over the entire test when you get it. Carefully note the directions (e.g., you may need to answer only *some* of the essays). Allot the proper time for the relative value of each section of the test.

Circle or check the numbers of the harder questions. Leave them for later. Completing some of the easier questions will help you answer the more difficult ones.

Read the directions for **objective or multiple choice items**. Note that sometimes the prof wants the *best* answer from among several "good" answers. Begin by reading the stem of the question to see if you can predict the answer. Then read all the choices to see how they fit the stem and your predicted answer. Consider each as a true/false statement and eliminate the false ones. Here are some other hints.

- Long answers are often the correct ones.
- Look for questions with qualifiers like "always" and "never." They are usually not correct.
- If your test is teacher-made (versus computer-generated), look for the right answer among the middle choices (e.g., B or C) rather than the first or last choices (e.g., A or D).
- For the more difficult test items, cross out any obviously wrong choices. Narrow down the choices as much as possible. If two choices are exactly opposite, one is probably the correct one.
- If you have trouble choosing, read the question and each choice as an independent statement. Grammatical agreement may tip you to the right choice. Your first guess is usually correct.
- Darken in circles later. Someone estimated it will save you five minutes per 100 questions.
- About every five questions, verify that you are marking the right line on the answer sheet.

The good news about **true-false** tests is that you have a 50 percent chance of guessing correctly. Try to justify your answers, stating to yourself why you know an item is true or an item is false. Here are some more tips.

- Note that many longer true/false statements and ones with qualifiers like "sometimes," "generally," and "usually" tend to be true. On the other hand, those with absolutes like "always" and "never" are typically false.
- Be careful with two-part statements. If one part is false, the entire statement is false.
- Watch out for double negative statements.
- If you are in doubt, it is better to guess "true" since true statements are easier for profs to write.

Fill-in test items are more difficult than multiple-choice and true-false items because they test your recall. Unlike essay questions, fill-in answers require precision, not writing around the issue with wordy sentences. For fill-in test items, write something in the blank even if you are not sure. The prof may give you some credit for creative thinking. If the answer is literally on the tip of your tongue, go through the alphabet letter-by-letter. It may trigger your memory.

Essay questions require you to know exactly what is being asked. Don't hesitate to ask your prof to clarify a confusing term or unclear question. Then, decide how much time you will spend on each essay, assigning more time to the essays that count the most.

- Spend a few minutes outlining your essay answer on scratch paper. Organization and neatness do count and impress. Some professors will lower your grade if your logic is confusing or they develop eyestrain trying to decipher your hieroglyphics.
- Then follow this time-honored advice: (1) *"Tell 'em what you're gonna tell 'em* (the introduction), (2) *Tell 'em* (the body), and (3) *Tell 'em what you told 'em"* (the conclusion).
- In the introduction, define your terms. In the body, make your best point first, use examples, and, if possible, quote your professor. (In general, on tests you should agree with the viewpoints expressed by your prof. Use class discussions for controversial opinions that contradict what your prof is advocating.) In the conclusion, quickly summarize your points.
- You should always strive for partial credit, even if you draw a complete mental blank. Try to write *something*. Compassionate professors or their graduate assistants will often give you partial credit.

When you get the test back, take the time to review it for errors. Learn from your mistakes. Is there a pattern to them? Did you misread questions? Did you fail to budget your time? If you don't understand why points were taken off, be sure to ask your professor or the TA. Teaching assistants especially want to help students improve, so don't be afraid to set up an appointment to go over your test if you are unclear about anything. Save returned tests to study from for the final exam. Some profs love to repeat questions.

Coping with Test Anxiety

Test-taking is stressful and unavoidable. However, some anxiety-reducing measures can help.

First, know where you stand in the course to help you put a given test in perspective. For example, if your outstanding past test performance allowed you to "bank" points, you don't need to get overanxious about how you might do on the current test. Or if you know you have a B going into a test, you can relax. If you've studied hard, you probably won't jeopardize that grade. Being semi-relaxed and well prepared might even help you perform well enough to raise your course grade to an A.

Be sure to gather what you need for the test the night before: pens, a calculator, watch, student ID, bluebook. You don't want to have to locate test materials frantically on your way to class. Your nerves will be frayed enough already.

Next, be sure to arrive to class early, but not too early. Choose a good seat, away from drafty windows and long-winded friends. In fact, it's a good idea to avoid your other classmates altogether. Their pre-test chit-chat and last-minute cramming can prove to be a distraction.

When you receive the test, divide your time according to the relative value of each section of the test. Ignore the test-taking pace of others. Some people flip pages quickly because they are totally lost and anxious to leave the testing room.

If you freeze up, take a deep breath to relax. Then proceed to answer the easy questions first for a boost of confidence. Remind yourself that you are going to be demonstrating what you *know*, not what you don't know. And always strive for partial credit by writing *something* down if at all possible.

Don't leave the testing room early. Review the test items if you finish ahead of time. For example, retake the objective items, covering your original answers. You may catch a few mistakes.

Finally, keep the test in perspective. You've studied your best and given the test your complete effort. Let the test go. How well or poorly you did ultimately has little cosmic significance. For example, picture yourself 70 years from now on your deathbed. I seriously doubt that you will care how you did on a given test. When the test is over, move on to the next challenge in your life. Try not to give it another thought.

10 SMART THINGS COLLEGE FRESHMEN DO	10 DUMB THINGS COLLEGE FRESHMAN DO
Say "no" to many commitments	Get involved in too many activities
Plan ahead by stating realistic goals, outlining tasks needed to execute them, and finding a way to check progress	Refuse to set goals or make calendars
Have a regular study time and stick to it	Pull all-nighters
Go to class	Cut classes
Learn from mistakes on old exams	Toss old exams
Do extra work	Watch a lot of television
Work ahead	Procrastinate
Socialize as a reward for good study	Party during the week
Maintain a support system (linked with family)	Go it alone
Establish a relationship with profs	Never visit professors

Writing Papers

"Writing is easy. All you do is stare at a blank sheet of paper until drops of blood form on your forehead."
—GENE FOWLER

You will write many papers in college: themes, critical essays, reflections, reports, reaction papers, take-home exams, and of course, the infamous term papers. Each academic department has its own style of handling documentation in papers, and professors have their own individual quirks on how they want you to write papers for their classes. Attend to these departmental and professorial guidelines as a first step in writing an acceptable paper.

An equally important first step is to *start your papers early*. "Paper procrastination" is a common disease among college students. The problem is multiplied to dangerous degrees when dealing with term papers. The writing of a term paper requires that you identify a worthwhile topic, read a great deal of information, organize and synthesize discrete pieces of information, and report your quotes and sources in an intelligent, accurate, and disciplined manner. The purpose of a term paper is to teach you *how* to learn: to retrieve information, to develop critical thinking skills, and to integrate knowledge. In short, it is hard work, and that's why students procrastinate.

If you want to write good term papers with a minimum of tension, start early and get organized. First, create a timetable. Begin with a due date and work backwards. Next, identify a topic that would interest you or that you wish to learn more about. Browse your textbook and the library for potential topics. Also, search the Internet for other ideas. When you find a topic that you would like to research, read some general works to help you narrow your topic. Then check your library resources and the Internet to see if there is enough relevant and up-to-date information on your topic. If so, you are ready to begin your research.

Write up a preliminary thesis statement to help you narrow your research. Now begin gathering your information. Take accurate notes on 4" x 6" index cards that you can easily arrange and rearrange as you create and revise your outline. These notes become the main source of information for your paper. Be sure to keep track of all your sources on 3" x 5" index cards. You will need these later to construct your footnotes and Works Cited page.

Next, develop an outline with headings and subheadings for major divisions. Use these headings when you write your paper to break up long pages of type and to reveal to the reader your logic and organization. Headings and subheadings will help to solve this problem.

After assembling and organizing your information into an outline, you are prepared to begin your first draft. Compose all stages of your paper on your computer. This enables you to revise your work easily, format footnotes automatically, and check spelling and grammar.

A prime advantage to starting your term papers early is that you can put your first draft aside for a few days before rewriting it. Always rewrite and revise several times if you want your paper to stand out. For too many students, their first draft is their *final* draft. Profs easily recognize this type of effort. Giving your paper a fresh look after a few days can help you make effective refinements. An early start will also allow you to get a classmate to read and critique a first and other drafts. Finding a friend with whom to swap and proofread papers is an incomparable gift for aspiring writers of any ability level.

Another plus to an early term-paper start is that you will have time to ask the prof or grad assistant for help. You will also have the opportunity to go to the writing lab without the pressure of an imminent deadline weighing you down.

Before submitting your final draft, make sure you have carefully created your bibliography or Works Cited page. Reread your paper to make sure that you avoided plagiarism, that is, using someone's exact words, original theories, and other information like graphs and charts, or paraphrased their ideas, without giving them due credit. Plagiarism is theft. Purchasing a paper online, copying pages of information without citing their source, and having a friend do a paper are all violations of academic integrity that have serious consequences at all colleges.

Finally, as columnist William Safire has reminded us, we should avoid bad grammar. His "Fumblerules of Grammar" should help you to this end:

- Don't use no double negatives.
- Proofread carefully to see if you any words out.
- Take the bull by the hand and avoid mixed metaphors.
- If I've told you once, I've told you a thousand times, resist hyperbole.
- Avoid commas, that are not necessary.
- Avoid clichés like the plague.
- Never use a long word when a diminutive will do.
- Avoid colloquial stuff.
- Verbs has to agree with their subject.

Challenges and Dilemmas of College Life   4

GOOD ADVICE FROM WISE ELDERS

"Watch your thoughts, for they become words. Choose your words, for they become actions. Understand your actions, for they become habits. Study your habits, for they will become your character. Develop your character, for it becomes your destiny."

—ANONYMOUS

"Never give in! Never give in! Never, never, never, never— in nothing great or small, large or petty. Never give in except to convictions of honor and good sense."

—WINSTON CHURCHILL

You will learn many things in college, some more helpful for your growth than others. Much of what you learn will indeed be forgotten. But the learning process and other college experiences will have a profound effect on the person you become. And most likely the challenges before you, and how you deal with them, will help form you as the kind of woman or man who will rise above the mediocrity that marks so many in our society. As Helen Keller so wisely observed, "Character cannot be developed in ease and quiet. Only through experiences of trial and suffering can the soul be strengthened, vision cleared, ambition inspired, and success achieved."

Your dogged determination to "never give in," wedded to a positive attitude of meeting challenges head-on, will help you handle some tough problems and decisions that inevitably are part of the college scene. This chapter focuses on some challenging issues you are likely to confront during your first year of college, including:

- Dealing with troublesome profs
- Deciding whether or not to pledge sororities or fraternities
- Handling dating, love, and sexual feelings in appropriate ways
- Understanding the ramifications of alcohol and drugs
- Responding to the widespread practice of cheating on college campuses

College Professors: Handle with Care

"A teacher affects eternity;
he can never tell where his influence stops."
—HENRY BROOKS ADAMS

Surveys of people's greatest fears include speaking in public, the fear of dying (which has intensified in recent years because of terrorist threats), and the fear of being rejected by others. Other top-ranking fears include getting fat, being around high or exposed places, and going to the dentist. To this list college students would often add: being stuck with a heartless, demanding, or unreasonable professor.

With luck, you won't get any professor with those characteristics during your college career and, if you do, you'll have the good sense to transfer out of his or her course while you have the time. To state once again, take advantage of your orientation session to find out from veteran students which profs to avoid. One further piece of advice: Don't always trust your freshman advisor to know who are the good profs. My daughter's freshman advisor, a competent English professor, recommended that she take a calculus course from the toughest teacher in the math department. The prof was a nice person, but very demanding on freshmen. My daughter didn't need a course like that during her very first semester at college. She "toughed it out," but many of her classmates dropped the course. She learned to seek out the opinions of more experienced students before enrolling in core courses taught by professors unknown to her.

Usually, you will enroll in courses with competent, fair, and knowledgeable profs. Sometimes, you will be fortunate enough to land some truly great professors. Experts in their field, they expect excellence from you and evoke it through their example rather than through intimidation. They are patient and empathetic. And they love the art of teaching, their subject matter, and students of all ability levels. When you run into professors like this, sign up for every course they offer. They make going to college exciting and mind-stretching.

You can work toward a good relationship with most college professors simply by observing common courtesies, including the following:

- *Address your professors by their correct title.* Some are very sensitive if you do not call them "Doctor" or "Professor." At times, you will find some profs who are informal and won't mind you calling them by their first name. But let them invite you to use this more casual approach.
- *Be on time for class.* Tardiness does not go unnoticed. It annoys and distracts lecturers. If you are going to be late, enter the room unobtrusively.
- *Read the syllabus and know course policies.* This will save misunderstandings down the line.
- *Participate in class discussions.* When appropriate, ask intelligent questions. Be attentive in class and show it by making eye contact. There is nothing more reassuring to a teacher than to have students who "connect" by paying attention and who give some type of feedback through good eye contact, occasionally nodding the head, or by asking a stimulating question.
- *When appropriate, compliment the professor for an outstanding lecture.* Cynics might call this "schmoozing" or, more crudely, "brown-nosing." More charitably, Christian decency requires that we acknowledge the superior contributions of others—peers or mentors.
- *Refuse to give excuses for late or inadequate work.* Lame rationalizations might have worked in high school, but college professors can see through transparent sophomoric excuses. There is no substitute for hard work, promptly delivered. Professors notice and reward such effort.
- A former student wrote with this excellent advice: *"Make sure*

you talk to your teacher if you are having problems—or even if you are not. Let them know you are interested in their class. This will often help you receive a better grade on the final report card."

- *Get to know the profs in your major field of study.* Remember that down the line in your academic career someone will have to write a letter of recommendation for you. You must know and befriend at least some of your professors. One way of doing this is to express an interest in a prof's research and ask to participate in some way. Many professors love to mentor students interested in their field of expertise.

FOUR THINGS YOUR PROFESSORS DON'T WANT TO HEAR

"Did I miss anything important in class yesterday?"	To the ears of professors, this question is like chalk screeching on a chalkboard. You are expected to attend every class. For them, each class is important, and they expect you to be interested in what they have to teach. If you are not, you must get motivated.
"Do we have to know this for the test?"	High-school kids ask this. Professors want you to think critically, to recognize what is important or not and how to organize it. Pay attention to each lecture and listen for the cues they give for what might be tested.
"But I was up all night writing this paper."	That's the problem. You should have started sooner and written more than one draft. If you are having trouble writing, be sure to go to the writing lab.
"Why did I get this grade?"	If you need to discuss your grade with a professor, make an appointment. While there, listen carefully and learn from your mistakes. Ask how you can improve for the next exam.

Following the above tips should help you maintain a good relationship with most of your professors, whether they are up-to-date experts or fossils in their field, great teachers or poor communicators, available or distant, parsimonious or generous graders, excited about teaching or bored with it.

However, as psychologist and veteran college teacher Christopher F. Monte warns, there are several types of professors who need special care if you are going to survive in their classes: the arrogant, the narcissistic, the indifferent, and the obsessive professors.[1] Ideally, you will transfer out of their classes. If this is impossible, Monte gives some good advice on how to recognize and cope with each of these professor types.

- *Arrogant* professors, Monte writes, have a distorted sense of their own achievement. They are insecure and must display their "superior" intelligence in order to be accepted. They are basically angry and don't like others to best them. These professors have a knack for angering their students. Work to keep your anger in check. Recognize that such professors have a poor self-image and are hurting inside because of their insecurity. They are not superior to you. A Christian response would be to be kind to these professors and respect what they can teach you. They probably have achieved some academic goal and can have something worthwhile to offer you. Avoid taking them for a future course.

- *Narcissistic* profs are sad, with very fragile and easily-wounded self-images. They are oversensitive to others' reactions to them. They are self-absorbed, self-focused, and hungry for love. They abhor competition from their students. Ignoring or snubbing narcissistic professors is dangerous. Listen carefully to them. Make eye contact. Be prepared for their mood shifts. Continue to be kind, loving, and respectful. They won't forget your consideration and will find a way to repay you.

- *Indifferent* profs, as described by Monte, are cold, aloof, apathetic, and cynical. They hate teaching and see it more as a job than a vocation. Intimacy for them provokes anxiety. They see learning as a detached interaction with neutral subject matter. Don't imitate indifferent professors' coolness toward the subject matter. Remember that the messenger is not equal to the message. Throw yourself into the readings to derive some real warmth from the subject area. If possible, switch courses.

- *Obsessive* profs are order and neatness freaks. They need organization, control, and exactness in every detail of the class. Their fanaticism about details, rigidity, and inflexibility both anger and numb students. It is important to follow the rules of obsessive professors. Be sure you always come to class and do so *promptly*. Meet their due dates. When you are confused about requirements, always ask for clarification. Avoid these kinds of teachers in the future.

To Pledge or Not to Pledge

"This above all: to thine own self be true."
—POLONIUS IN SHAKESPEARE'S *HAMLET*, I, III, 75

"To go Greek or not" . . . that is the question. It won't take long before you must decide whether to pledge a fraternity or sorority. This decision will greatly affect the quality of your entire college experience. Make it carefully, only after weighing all the pros and cons.

There are three main types of these student associations. *Professional* fraternities and sororities are open by invitation to students and faculty in a particular field of study, for example, law, journalism, or engineering. *Honor* societies are for distinguished scholars of outstanding character who live up to other requirements established by the particular association. The most distinguished honor society is Phi Beta Kappa.

Social fraternities and sororities, where membership is by invitation, promote the social purposes of their members. To join one of these involves a screening process called rushing, when you are approached or "rushed" by members about the possibility of joining. Rush Week can take place the summer before you go to college, but on many campuses it takes place early in the spring term when a candidate visits the prospective fraternity and sorority houses. To receive a bid (acceptance into particular association) requires the vote of each member. Thus, potential pledges must spend considerable time during Rush Week getting to know the members of the most desirable houses. If a candidate receives a bid and accepts, then he or she becomes a pledge. Pledges typically have to endure an initiation rite.

Unfortunately, initiation rites have led to serious incidents of hazing on some college campuses. Because some of these have led to injury and even death to new pledges, many colleges in the past decade or so have taken steps to outlaw, or severely restrict, Greek life on their campuses. College administrators at schools like Dartmouth have argued that fraternities and sororities contradict worthy institutional goals like coeducation, gender equality, and inclusiveness and, therefore, are out of step with the school's mission. The University of Notre Dame is a prominent college that does not have social fraternities or soroities.

Benefits of Membership

Why do college students join fraternities and sororities? The most common reason members give is instant camaraderie. Being a member of a Greek letter association promises members a new set of friends, a sense of belonging to a brotherhood or sisterhood, and an instantaneous social life. Many Greeks stay friends for life and provide each other with a solid base for professional networking after graduation. Academic fringe benefits include advice from older members concerning courses and profs, and access to a bank of books, old course notes, exams, quizzes, term papers and projects that can help the member survive college. Of course, drawing on these resources can often be cheating.

Today, an increasing number of Greek societies are attempting to fight the *Animal House* image, the perception that the organization's only purpose is to throw the best and wildest party on campus. Most Greek houses engage in worthwhile service projects that foster a sense of community while tapping into the idealism and goodness of college students who want to make a positive contribution in the service of others.

Drawbacks of Membership

A negative of joining a Greek letter society is that you might push away non-brothers or -sisters from your circle of friends. In addition, you must be willing to make an enormous commitment of time and energy for the various activities of the brotherhood or sisterhood. Members of fraternal organizations reported higher rates of academic dishonesty than non-Greeks. This is due in part to cutting class, not going to review sessions, and doing less study for tests because of the large amounts to time devoted to fraternity and sorority activities.[2] In addition, joining up also costs money, at least several hundred dollars each year.

There are some Christian soroities and fraternities but most are without religious affiliation. Too much partying, a tradition of hazing, and being a member of a closed society—all these contribute to the negative stereotyping of some Greek societies. The famed Harvard School of Public Health College Alcohol Study substantiated what many critics have always believed—that there is a strong correlation between fraternity membership and binge drinking. Subsequent studies have confirmed that those living in Greek houses are four times more likely to be binge drinkers than non-Greeks.[3] In addition, Greek brothers and sisters need to conform to the traditions, customs, and expectations of the group, thus surrendering a certain amount of individuality in the process.

Some of these negative generalizations may be more pronounced for a given fraternity or sorority on your campus. If you are even remotely considering joining a fraternity or sorority, be sure to answer for yourself or inquire of others the answers to these questions:

- Do you have the same interests as a good majority of the fraternity or sorority members in question?
- What is the GPA of the members? (Hanging around with good students is bound to have a positive effect.)
- How long does it take the average Greek brother or sister to graduate from college? (If it is five or six years, you may want to question why.)
- How much are the annual dues? Can you afford them?
- How much time must you devote to your Greek sisters or brothers? Will the time and other commitments distract you from the main purpose of college—getting an education?
- Are positive things going on with this association? Will membership in it make you a better person?
- What are the living conditions like, especially for new pledges? What house duties will you have to perform?
- What is the purpose of the initiation? Is it dehumanizing or is it just harmless fun?
- Is this something you really want to do, or are you getting "rushed" into it?

Recommendation: The first-year of college is a time of adjustment. If you have an intense desire to join a Greek letter society, spend your first year studying the various options to be sure you find one that is worthy of your own high values. Wait until the spring term of your sophomore year before you agree to pledge.

Dating, Love, and Sex

"So live that you wouldn't be ashamed to sell the family parrot to the town gossip."
—WILL ROGERS

A real advantage to college life is the opportunity to develop, nurture, and cherish mature friendships with all kinds of people of both genders. Being in class with other young, intelligent persons of the opposite sex can be a real eye opener, especially if you attended a same-sex high school or you were shy around the opposite sex during your high-school years.

In college, make it a top priority to develop opposite-sex friendships built on equality, mutual respect, and open communication. A big step to poise and adult maturity is the ability to relate in friendship to the other half of the human race. Seize every opportunity to converse with members of the other sex by chatting before class, eating meals together in mixed groups, joining study groups, participating in an extracurricular activity, attending concerts and movies, and dating.

Making Friends First

A good rule of thumb is to make friends first with members of the opposite sex before you begin any "serious" dating. You will, of course, want to date in college, and you should when the opportunity presents itself. However, the nature of dating in our society too quickly narrows the field and closes you off to other opposite-sex friendships. Note the contrast: friendship includes others; dating tends to be exclusive. Friendship is open and public; dating leans toward togetherness and privacy. Friendship is social and interpersonal while avoiding the trappings and pitfalls of romance; dating can move closer and closer to self-absorption, possessiveness, and jealousy. As C. S. Lewis observed in *The Four Loves*, "Lovers are normally face to face, absorbed in each other; friends, side by side, absorbed in some common interest."

Meeting and befriending members of the opposite sex as equals is freeing. It liberates the male especially from the societal stereotype of the individual conqueror who wins by dominating women. Having friendships with women can remind men that females are persons deserving of profound respect, not because of their external appearance, but because they possess inner beauty and worth as God's creation.

College Romance Today

The sexual revolution, jump-started in the 1960s, has created a whole different way for males and females to relate on today's college campuses. In the past, colleges and universities assumed the parental role of guardianship that helped guide college students to engage in responsible behavior as they grew into adulthood. Today, colleges have surrendered the policy of *in loco parentis*, leaving students pretty much on their own to figure out affairs of the heart.

In the view of some social commentators, the ritual of dating on college campuses is dying a fast death. Leon Kass wrote, "Today, there are no socially prescribed forms of conduct that help guide young men and women in the direction of matrimony."[4]

In the past, dating in college typically took place with the view of finding a marriage partner. Today, the overriding goal of college is preparation for a future career with little encouragement for settling down soon after graduation. However, this state of affairs does not mean college students are abstaining from sex. Growing up in our sex-saturated environment, you are probably not too shocked to learn that many college-age men and women engage in sexual relationships without any sense of commitment.

A recent survey of one thousand college women confirmed what my own children learned about the death of the dating scene on college campuses today.[5] The survey revealed that only 50 percent of the female college seniors had been asked out on more than six dates during their entire college career. And one-third in the survey had been asked on no more than two dates.

The survey reported that male-female relationships on today's campuses involve "hooking up," "hanging out," or "being joined at the hip." Dating in the traditional sense of the word was a distant fourth among the available options. Despite the hype of today's feminists, fewer than 40 percent of the young women interviewed were happy with this social scene on campus.

"Hooking up" is a practice that allows sexual interaction ("ranging from kissing to having sex") without commitment or even affection. According to the research study, freshman women hook up the most, notably because of the attention they get, often from junior and senior guys. A notable feature of hook-ups is that they typically happen when both the guy and the girl have been drinking. Reasons given for hook-ups include stress release, feeling in control, and using sex to counteract depression.

Hooking up differs from past courtship patterns where it was the man's role to risk rejection when asking a woman out on a date. A major goal was for him to make a good impression on her. It was then the woman's prerogative to pursue the relationship or not. In the traditional view of dating, there was no implication that the couple would have an enduring relationship or that it would lead to sex.

Men and women would date several persons at a time with the view of having fun while learning to develop civilizing social skills. It had unwritten rules and expectations, for example, that it was rude for a man to ask a woman on a date at the last minute. Dating was (and is) an honorable way to grow into responsible, respectful, and loving relationships with members of the opposite sex.

College students think of dating in ways other than the traditional one just described. The first is being "joined at the hip" where a man and woman meet and quickly form a serious and intense bond that results in sexual intimacy. They agree that they will not see other people and spend almost every waking minute together.

A second type of "dating" is rare. It resembles "joined at the hip," but moves more slowly. The man and woman see each other several times a week, but agree not to "see" anyone else. They go out with their friends, maintaining a college life that exists apart from their own one-on-one relationships. Basically, the couple is "going slow" in their relationship, but they still want it to be exclusive. Their motivation for doing so is often due to the religious values they have.

A third type of dating is the traditional date in which the man invites the woman out, picks her up, and pays for the date. As noted above, only half of the senior women reported having more than six dates, in this traditional sense, during their four years of college.

A fourth and most common form of dating on college campuses today is "hanging out." This has a variety of meanings including spending time with the opposite sex, viewing movies together in dorm rooms, and studying together in the library. Men possibly engage in this type of "dating" pattern to hide their interest in a woman for fear of rejection or because they fear a deeper level of commitment than they want to get involved in at the time.

Interestingly, many of the women in the study said coed dorms have helped create the climate of today's campus by facilitating casual sexual relations. One of the main pluses for separate dorms is that it would be easier for couples to break up if they were not living under the same roof.

Dating Tips

Knowing college dating patterns on today's campuses should help if you have never had the opportunity to date in high school. Even if you have dated before, as you enter college no one will know (or care) about your high-school background with its failures and successes. As you begin your college career, resolve to meet and date a variety of people. It is good to "play the field," even if you have left a boyfriend or girlfriend behind. (Recall that it is not a good idea to promise that you won't even meet and interact with a variety of people of the opposite sex while at college, let alone date others.) Now is the time in your life to befriend and date many people to widen your experiences and grow as a person. If your hometown relationship is the "real thing," dating in college won't destroy it.

"Hanging out" may be the way you will begin to interact with members of the opposite sex at the start of your college career. It is a relatively safe way to get to know others and develop friendships. Be sure to engage in meaningful conversations. Showing a genuine interest in others—their families, majors, likes and dislikes—leads to the kind of self-revelation that may encourage you to begin dating in a more traditional sense.

As you develop a deeper relationship with someone, build it on openness and honesty. If someone is going to fall in love with you, you want to make sure he or she knows the *real* you. This means being up-front about your religious and ethical values. Ideally, you will attract and find attractive a person whose moral standards and religious beliefs support and nurture your own, for example, someone who is:

- kind (that is, thoughtful and loving)
- honest
- intelligent
- loyal
- considerate (concerned about *you* and *your* interests)
- interesting (multidimensional)
- empathetic
- affectionate (open to giving and receiving compliments; warm)
- possessing a good sense of humor
- principled (a person of integrity)

Find these qualities in a potential dating companion, and you will have found someone who is bound to make you a better person.

Sex in the News

To state the obvious, we live in a sex-saturated world. Note the following news reports of interest to college students:

- An ABC News story reports on a survey conducted by the Society for Adolescent Medicine. It found that 56 percent of the college students who live away from home had been sexually active while attending college. Of this group, 73 percent said they engaged in unprotected sex while in college. About two-thirds of those who had unprotected sex did not believe they were at risk for sexually transmitted diseases.[6]
- The Centers for Disease Control and Prevention reports that chlamydia is the most common bacterially transmitted STD in the United States, estimating that there were some three million new cases in 2000. About 85 percent of females who contract this disease are symptom-free, thus creating a "hidden epidemic" that can cause sterilization because of scarring in the fallopian tubes.[7]
- "Approximately 40,000 new HIV infections occur each year in the United States, about 70 percent among men and 30 percent among women. Of these newly infected people, half are younger than 25 years of age."[8]

- By age 24, one in three sexually active people will have contracted an STD—and many may not realize when they become infected.[9]
- One in five abortions are performed on college women.[10]

Your College and Sex

As noted above, with the demise of *in loco parentis*, don't look for your college to supervise your sexual behavior. Freshman orientation may include sessions on date rape, alcohol abuse, and "safe sex," but there is little attempt subsequently to monitor what students do on their own time. Coed dorms, few if any rules about after-hours room visitation, and the lack of a curfew all convey the message that students are on their own when managing their sexual behavior.

As a college student, your sex drive is at its peak or near-peak. With all the beautiful young people on campus, it is not unusual to have sex on the mind a good deal of the time. Sexual thoughts are natural and normal. They are only wrong when they become lustful, that is, deliberately engaged in to inflame your desires past the boundaries that God has set for healthy and moral sexual attraction. Also, having sexual thoughts and feelings does not mean a person *must* act on them. Of course, today's popular society assumes that you will, that you cannot (or should not) resist your sexual urges. Colleges often convey this same message, for example, by placing condom machines in dorm restrooms.

Your classmates and dormmates will have various thoughts about premarital sex. Some of them have decided to abstain from sex until marriage. Others are confused, undecided, and wavering. Still others are sexually active with one partner or promiscuously active with many partners.

You will hear many reasons for why you should be having sex; among the most prevalent is peer pressure—everyone else is doing so, why not you? Your sexual orientation or level of "maturity" may be questioned if you are not having sex. The reality is that freedom from parental rules + raging hormones + the message that sexual experience before marriage is inevitable + many peers who habitually and without question indulge in sex all add up to powerful temptations to engage in sex in college.

Sexual Intercourse Is for Marriage

We live in a society that tolerates and even promotes sexual activity without commitment. The only message that is preached is that when you have sex, either with members of the opposite or same sex, just be sure it is "safe" sex. The message of self-indulgence without commitment has led to a host of problems, not the least of which is the breakdown of the family upon which healthy and moral societies are built.

Sexual intercourse is the fullest expression of sexual sharing between a man and a woman. Christians see sex as our profoundest form of communication with deep human meaning. Sexual intercourse is body language that signifies the love of one spouse for the other in a total gift of self. It says: "I am giving you my entire self, completely and exclusively. Through this act, I declare my total commitment to you."

True love and lasting commitment are the bottom-line reasons why sexual intercourse is to be reserved for marriage. In marriage, a couple has publicly promised exclusive and mutual self-giving "for better or for worse, in sickness and in health," as long as both shall live. This unbreakable promise creates a stable relationship that can nourish the couple's love and provide the proper context for the raising of children. There is no way for this promise to be made (and kept) between a man and woman outside of marriage.

To use the language of love outside of marriage misuses the profound and beautiful symbol of communication. To do so is to be dishonest and untrue to self. Sexual lovemaking should speak the language of full commitment. In contrast, an unmarried couple can always bail out of their relationship because they have not really given themselves totally to each other.

Saving sex until marriage is the right choice because sexual intercourse symbolizes and expresses the permanent commitment of true love. Couples who invoke the word "love" in their premarital unions are involved in self-deception. Psychology shows that sexual intimacy before marriage is all too often a front for manipulation, possessiveness, anger, escape, and a host of other emotional problems. Broken relationships always cause hurt. And misusing sex is a source of great emotional and spiritual hurt when the relationship ends.

What unmarried men and women need in their relationship is pre-marital *love*. Remember, St. Paul lists *patience* as the first quality of love (see 1 Corinthians 13). True love waits for marriage to have sex.

Benefits of Living Chastely

Christian teaching calls college students, and everyone else, to live the virtue of chastity. This means that everyone must conform his or her sexual behavior to a particular state in life. Married people must abstain from sexual relations with everyone but their spouse. A non-married college student must abstain from sexual intercourse until marriage. Living chastely is incredibly freeing, bringing with it a host of benefits. For example:

- You will have a clear conscience and a right relationship with God because you will be living in harmony with his plan for your future.
- You will be disease free. (Abstinence is 100 percent safe. Despite media hype, there is no other form of "safe" sex. Living chastely will inoculate you from more than fifty STDs, including AIDS. And you won't have to worry about condoms failing, which they do at least 10 percent of the time.)
- You won't get pregnant or be responsible for a pregnancy that may derail your college or career plans. You won't have to consider abortion or a premature decision to marry.
- You will save yourself great anxiety and worry over the *possibilities* of catching a disease or having a baby. Worry makes you neglect your studies, thus endangering your academic career.
- You will treat yourself and others with respect.
- You will learn the self-control that you will need in all aspects of life. Your future marriage will require discipline for you and your spouse to remain faithful through "thick and thin."
- You are free from playing sexual games. As a result, you can redirect your positive energy to worthwhile pursuits like sports and various service projects.
- You will make a positive countercultural statement about chastity and abstinence to refute today's conventional wisdom that reduces humans to sexual animals or programmed machines. You will witness to the dignity of persons as free, loving, and intelligent beings who *can* control themselves.

- You will have the time and freedom to build true friendships. Lasting marriages are built on friendship. Sex is only part of the formula for marriage, albeit a very good part. A chaste lifestyle will free you to find a potential mate who is like-minded and willing to accept you for the person that you are.

How to Handle and Avoid Sexual Temptations

Remaining chaste and abstaining from sexual relations before marriage requires you to decide right now. It is a decision that includes these actions:

1. *Stay close to Jesus.* Unless you are an angel (a spirit without a body), you will need Jesus' help to master sexual temptations. Jesus calls us to high standards. To follow him is often difficult, but he promised that he would help his friends. Ask for God's help in this area, both in private prayer and in the weekly worship.
2. *Choose like-minded friends.* We all need a support group that will nurture, not undermine, our values.
3. *Be sure your date knows your standards.* No one has the right to demand sex because money was spent on you. Say "no" firmly and strongly if your date begins to pressure you for sex. You are not required to share your reasons for saying "no."
4. *Know where to draw the line.* Drawing the line means staying sober. Drugs and alcohol lower inhibitions and resolve. Alcohol abuse is implicated in many date rapes.

   Drawing the line means avoiding tempting situations. Sex is beautiful, exciting, passionate, and progressive. Once sexual passion kicks into gear, it yearns for greater intimacy and union. Avoid situations and places that will lower your resolve, for example, drinking and being alone together in an isolated place, including a dorm room.

   Drawing the line means dressing modestly. You don't want to send the wrong message.

   Drawing the line means properly handling displays of affection. For example, prolonged open-mouthed kissing and petting comprise the slippery slope to the full sexual expression of intercourse. Limit your show of affection to hand holding, hugs, and light kissing.

   Drawing the line means avoiding sexually suggestive movies and conversations. These inflame sexual desires and lead to improper behavior.

Remember, the feeling of *wanting* to have sex does not mean you have to have sex. As a human being with freedom, you *can* control your behavior.

To Party or Not

"All excess is ill, but drunkenness is of the worst sort. It spoils health, dismounts the mind, and unmans men. It reveals secrets, is quarrelsome, lascivious, impudent, dangerous and bad."
—WILLIAM PENN (1644–1718)

In the popular mind, college students and partying are synonymous. The enduring popularity of a film like *Animal House* which extols partying and drinking into oblivion perpetuates the myth that college years are primarily for getting drunk or getting high. Unfortunately, some students, including many college freshmen, live that myth. The consequences can be tragic.

Binge drinking is a serious problem. A binge drinker is defined as a person who consumes five or more drinks in a row for males and four or more drinks in a row for females.[11] A study by Harvard University's School of Public Health College Alcohol Study found the following:

- 44 percent of U.S. college students engaged in binge drinking during the two weeks before the survey
- 51 percent of the men drank five or more drinks in a row; 40 percent of the women drank four or more drinks in a row
- Over half of the binge drinkers, almost one in four students, were frequent binge drinkers, that is, they binged *three or more times* in a two-week period.[12]

Another recent study by the National Institute on Alcohol Abuse and Alcoholism found that binge drinking causes 1,400 deaths, 500,000 injuries, and 70,000 cases of sexual assault or date rape each year. The same study found that the drinking rates were highest among *incoming freshmen*, males, athletes, and fraternity and sorority members.[13]

Another finding reveals that one in ten students said they had unprotected sex while drinking.[14]

Setting Limits

Inebriation is wrong because it dehumanizes. It diminishes or destroys one's capacity to think rationally. It lessens or extinguishes will power. People who drink beyond the point of control typically get physically sick. In addition, they always get morally ill, causing harm to self and others. For example, three out of four college students report at least one bad consequence of another's drinking during the past school year. These include sleep or study being interrupted (71 percent), the need to take care of the drunk student (57 percent), being insulted or humiliated (36 percent), or experiencing an unwanted sexual advance (23 percent).[15]

Decide ahead of time what you are going to do about partying with alcohol and other drugs. Your advance decision is the ounce of prevention you'll need to protect yourself against the temptations of peer pressure. Be proactive. Draw the line now. Here are some related guidelines to consider:

- Avoid chemicals as a way to deal with stress. Never begin using them; not even once. If you are dealing with an issue you cannot handle, go to the student life or campus health center or Newman center chaplain and ask for help. Do it *now*!
- Don't allow others to pressure you. Avoid high-pressure situations where it is considered macho or cool to drink as much as possible as quickly as possible. If you must drink, nurse a drink over a long period of time. Also, be aware of the size of the drink you pour.
- If you want to try drugs, then leave college! Ask yourself: Do you know anyone who is a better student because he or she is on drugs? Are they better problem-solvers because of their addiction to drugs? Papers written while high that seem creative at first are mostly nonsensical or disjointed when the drugs wear off.
- If you must drink, devise a buddy system where another person looks out for you (and you for the other person). Signal each other when you have reached the limit. Know your limit. Know your partner's limit.
- If you or any friends will be going to or from a party in a car, *always* have a designated driver. You are socially irresponsible and deviant if you don't follow this most basic rule. You also have a death wish or prison wish for yourself or others. Yes,

countless college students die in alcohol-related car accidents. Yes, many college students—when driving while intoxicated—kill and maim innocent people.

- If your roommate is doing drugs, speak up and show him or her where to get help. If this doesn't work, talk to your RA. If you get no satisfaction, change roommates as soon as possible. People on drugs are dangerous to themselves and others. At the least, he or she will bring down your academic performance and social possibilities.
- If you are underage, consider the question of how you are going to break the law to obtain liquor. Will you have to lie (false ID) to do so? What policy, if any, does your college have if you get caught breaking the law? Consider: Is drinking *that* important to you?
- Be your own person. Some things are wrong. Can you stand up to peer pressure? Will you?
- *Never* drink anything from a punch bowl. You don't know what is in the concoction or what has been added to the mix. Never leave a drink unattended.
- Do you find vomiting and passing out attractive? This is one of the common results of binge drinking, especially among underage drinkers. You can bet many of them don't look or smell too attractive the next day.
- If you are taking any kind of medication, don't drink. The combination could be lethal.
- If you are drinking all the time, you have a problem. Get help now before it ruins your college career and your life.
- Moderation in everything!

We can all tell stories about how the abuse of alcohol in college has ruined lives. I personally know of former students who drowned or died in car accidents after college-drinking episodes. I know one young man who went to prison for sexual assault while intoxicated. I know a student who, when drunk, fell down a stairwell. He is permanently disabled today. I know another who contracted HIV because of his promiscuous sexual behavior while under the influence of alcohol. Sadly, I can think of several students who fit each of these tragic categories.

The most common fallout among my former students, however, has been the literally hundreds who were not able to handle the new-found freedom of the first year of college. "Free at last," they let loose with the drinking and began to party almost constantly. The results were very predictable: flunking out of college either after the first semester or most certainly by the end of the first year. Then, if lucky, off they went to a junior college to get back on track. Maybe after a year, they enrolled at a state college near to home. Most never made it back to their dream college.

There are some bright spots as more and more colleges ban alcohol at public events and increasing numbers of fraternities and sororities outlaw alcohol from all gatherings held in their chapter houses and in their pledge recruitment policies. Police in college towns have cracked down more strenuously by more rigorous enforcement of underage drinking and public intoxication laws. And many colleges are setting in place policies to control drinkers who are also date rapists, drunken drivers, slobs, vomiting roommates, clowns who pull dorm fire alarms at 4:00 a.m., and campus brawlers.

SAVE A LIFE

You must intervene immediately if a friend or acquaintance is suffering from *acute alcohol poisoning*.
- If you can't wake the person, or if he or she does not wake up during or after vomiting, check to see if his or her skin is cold, clammy, or unusually pale or bluish. Check the person's breathing. If it is slow or irregular (less than eight times a minute), act immediately.
- Call 911. Your friend's life is on the line.
- Stay with the person. Continue to try to wake him or her. Turn the person on his or her side to avoid choking if he or she begins vomiting.
- If the person stops breathing, start CPR. If you don't know how to, try to find someone who does.[16]

Cheating

"There is no pillow as soft as a good conscience."
—ANONYMOUS

Honesty is in short supply. Almost on a monthly basis, the media reports on corporate schemes that have caused major shockwaves to our economy. Unscrupulous accountants, lawyers, CEOs, and others falsify company reports, take advantage of insider trading, and engage in other illegal and unethical practices that have destroyed their companies, thrown thousands of innocent workers out of their jobs, and defrauded stockholders of hundreds of millions of dollars.

In addition, the political discourse in our country is at an all-time low. The level of hostility among people of varying political views is frightening. This is partly caused by the cultural war in which our society is engaged and the clash of values it produces. It is exacerbated by the mistrust engendered by politicians who lie about their personal behavior or who exaggerate claims to further their political agendas or who, to get elected, make empty promises to pander to particular interest groups.

Dishonesty in academics is also a serious problem in our society. It serves as a breeding ground for the epidemic of the unethical behaviors described above. Known as "intellectual theft," academic dishonesty takes many forms: copying test answers from classmates, using crib notes for exams, misusing calculators by preprogramming formulas to use during tests, purchasing papers from Internet term-paper services, failing to cite sources or fabricating quotes in term papers, cut-and-paste plagiarism, securing exams from accomplices, sabotaging the work of other students, and more.

Another form of college-level dishonesty involves athletic programs. Various scandals have been reported in recent years that involve players, coaches, and even top-ranking university officials. Grade-fixing, special treatment in test-taking, cash changing hands, and generous gift-giving undermine the academic integrity of our institutions of higher education.[17]

Plagiarism.org, an online resource to help educators stem Internet cheating, cites some statistics about cheating in college:

- almost 80 percent of college students admit to cheating at least once (from a study by The Center for Academic Integrity);
- 36 percent of undergraduates admit to plagiarizing written material (from a survey by the *Psychological Record*);
- 90 percent of students say that cheaters are never caught or disciplined appropriately (from a *US News and World Reports* poll).[18]

Students cheat for many reasons: sheer laziness, heavy work loads, lack of interest in the subject matter of required courses, and pressure to get good grades versus getting a good education. Most students who cheat have low self-esteem. The false grade their cheating results in enhances their self-image because they now believe others think more highly of them.

A major reason why basically honest students cheat is because their classmates cheat and get away with it. (Cheaters are rarely caught. Many professors do not rigorously enforce their schools' cheating policy.) Normally honest students believe they must succumb to cheating simply to survive. In addition, non-cheaters do not report cheating because they see it as the professors' job or are reluctant to judge the motives of the cheaters. As someone wisely observed, today's ethical system has created an 11th commandment—"Thou Shalt Not Judge Another." The result: cheating grows like a cancer.

Our society also strongly endorses the quick-fix solution cheating provides. We live in an era of instant gratification. Ads promise immediate success, social acceptance, and financial well-being—as long as we buy their products. The goal is to get ahead, and if cheating works, then why not?

According to popular culture, the major sin involved with cheating is not the act itself, but getting caught. When asked why he gambled while managing the Cincinnati Reds, baseball star Pete Rose said that he did not think he would get caught. His gambling—an offense severely condemned by professional baseball—barred Rose, the all-time hit king—from election to the Baseball Hall of Fame. "If you cheat, fine; but don't get caught. That's stupid." Today, the end justifies the means.

Temptations to cheat, to plagiarize, to pass off another's work as your own will meet you at every turn throughout your college career. Remember the advice of a college mathematics professor who said to his class:

> Today, I am giving two exams: one in calculus, the other in honesty. My hope is that you will pass both. If you are going to fail one, fail calculus. There are many good people in the world who are lost solving calc problems. But there are no good people in the world who cannot pass the test of honesty.

Personal integrity is the touchstone of character. It is in short supply today. As a Christian, your commitment to simple, basic honesty will be a resounding witness to your peers. In the words of Alexander Pope, "An honest [person] is the noblest work of God."

Your nobility will shine forth if you follow three basic rules:

- Don't cheat.
- Submit your own work. (This means not buying an online term paper, paying for someone to write your paper, or borrowing a paper from another student to submit as your own.)
- Don't plagiarize. (In your papers, give credit to others' work including their theories, ideas, and quotes. Cite your source if you copy paragraphs, sentences, or even phrases from another.)

In conclusion, consider the words of Abraham Lincoln who said:

> I am not bound to win, but I am bound to be true. I am not bound to succeed, but I am bound to live up to the light I have. I must stand with anybody that stands right, stand with him while he is right, and part with him when he goes wrong.[19]

Keeping Physically and Spiritually Fit

5

BASIC TRUTHS TO REMEMBER

I. Take your days one at a time.
II. Nothing wastes more energy than worry.
III. If you want your dreams to come true, don't oversleep.
IV. Don't learn safety rules by accident.
V. Jumping to conclusions can be bad exercise.
VI. Most of the answers you need are within you.
VII. The happiness of your life depends on the quality of your thoughts.
VIII. Not getting what you want is sometimes a great stroke of luck.
IX. The best vitamin for making friends . . . B1.
X. Ideas won't work unless you do.

This final chapter highlights ways to develop and maintain healthy habits by providing some coping techniques for physical, psychological, and spiritual fitness during your college years. The Romans had an expression, *mens sana in corpore sano*, "a healthy mind in a healthy body." This ancient wisdom is worth adopting. Many psychologists and spiritual advisors know well the link between a positive mental outlook and physical and psychological well-being, as the ten truths above express.

The topics in this chapter should be incorporated in your overall plan for college success:

- Healthy eating
- Sensible exercise
- Safety on campus
- Stress reduction
- Maintenance of spiritual health

Healthy Eating

"Dietary self-control is the capacity to break a chocolate bar in half, smell its heavenly aroma, and then eat just one piece."
—SOME GOOD ADVICE

College freshmen usually have a love-hate relationship with the food service at their school. They love the dining room because it is a great place to meet friends, unwind, and socialize. Also, most food plans allow you to go back for unlimited quantities of food. At home, you may have been limited to one helping of dessert. Not at college! You will find that no one will mind if you have an enormous mound of ice cream at every meal.

On the other hand, the *quality* of food on most campuses rarely receives high marks. You might find the daily main course mediocre at best. I recall that by the second semester of my freshman year I found the cafeteria food barely edible. Lots of late-night burgers and pizzas somehow sustained me until I moved off campus and did my own cooking.

The problem with readily available large quantities of food and late-night eating is the infamous "Freshman 15." Many frosh are surprised when they go home for Thanksgiving or Christmas break to discover that they have put on considerable weight, up to fifteen pounds. Clothes fit more tightly, and that svelte, lean look has quickly disappeared. When your mom starts making comments about your weight, you know it is time to take stock of your college eating habits.

Surveys tell us that more than half of college students have changed their eating behavior from home to school, often resulting in skipping meals, snacking frequently, eating foods high in fat, and not getting enough fruits, vegetables, or variety.[1] These newly acquired habits are like a comfortable bed—easy to get into, but hard to get out of. College is tough enough without lugging extra weight around. Start on the right foot, and you will save yourself the struggle to lose unwanted pounds during the second semester. Consider the following tips for a healthy, balanced diet.

Eat three modest-sized meals each day.

Avoid the fast-and-binge cycle. Consuming three meals, even if one meal is light, dulls sudden hunger surges and spreads out your energy level during the day. Binge eating is what adds those extra pounds. Eat a variety of foods from the basic food groups: milk, meat, fruits and vegetables, and grains. Substitute as necessary; for example, if you are a vegetarian make sure to supplement with other non-meat protein items, for example, peanut butter and beans.

Always eat breakfast.

Like your mom says, "Breakfast is the most important meal of the day." In the college cafeteria, breakfast may the best-tasting meal. It's almost impossible to ruin bacon, eggs, and pancakes. However, you should plan to indulge in these greasy foods only once or twice a week. Also avoid sugared cereals, donuts, and pastries. Too many sugary foods will cause an afternoon crash and the need for another sugar "fix" to get you through the day. Rather, eat cereal and toasted breads with fiber. Low-sugared jellies on low-fat bagels and muffins will satisfy your sweet tooth. Breakfast is a great time to stock up on Vitamin C. Be sure to eat a banana, orange, or grapefruit and drink plenty of fruit juices.

Veg out for lunch.

Your mother was also right when she told you that vegetables are good for you. The midday meal is a good time to hit the salad bar. It's always a pain to eat salads when you have to cut up and wash the vegetables yourself. The beauty of salad bars is that the hard work is already done for you. Watch your fat intake by using a low-fat dressing. Supplement the salad with a good low-fat soup when it is available and a piece or two of whole wheat bread. If you are in doubt about what to eat, research shows that a high-protein versus a high-carbohydrate lunch increases afternoon alertness.

If you think you might miss lunch, carry along an extra piece of fruit, a bagel, or sandwich in your knapsack. If you starve yourself in the afternoon, you're likely to overeat at dinner. Also, instead of a steady diet of sweetened soda pop, drink flavored mineral water, fruit juice, herbal tea, or just plain water. By the way, drinking eight glasses of water every day is not only healthy advice, it is also a great way to keep you from overeating. Your stomach can only handle so much volume.

Eat sensibly at dinner.

Avoid foods with too much fat, saturated fat, and cholesterol. Eat grilled chicken and fish whenever possible. They are low in fat and cholesterol. Cut the fat away from other meats. Also avoid too much sugar and sodium (salt) intake. A balanced diet should also include adequate starch and fiber. Baked potatoes are a good source of starch, and pastas are usually a great nutritional bargain. Try to eat at least one serving of vegetables at every meal. Limit yourself to one dessert. The key at dinnertime is to eat slowly, drink plenty of fluids, and resist the urge to go back for seconds.

Despite the presence of good, nutritional (but admittedly not always tasty) food on college campuses, fast food still rules the day for many students. Burgers, pizza, fries, tacos, and donuts *are* the meal plan for many college students seven days a week. It's okay to have fun and occasionally have a junk-food snack to break up a late-night study session; but always remember that those foods are high in fat and calories. Translation: extra weight, sluggishness, and potential health problems. If you know you'll be up late working on a term paper, stock your dorm refrigerator and shelves with some low-fat snacks (e.g., fruit, popcorn without butter, carrots).

Caffeine is a drug to which many college students become addicted in the form of coffee, tea, soft drinks, chocolate, and over-the-counter brand-name products like NoDoz.™ A moderate intake of caffeine is habit-forming. However, over-consumption of caffeine can lead to insomnia, nervousness, anxiety, intestinal disorders, and increased urination that can cause dehydration.

As covered before, alcohol consumption does not make for a good student. The Department of Health and Human Services offers a reminder that if you drink alcoholic beverages, do so in moderation. Alcoholic beverages supply calories, but little or no nutrients. Drinking alcohol is also the cause of many health problems and accidents and can lead to addiction.[2]

Beware of eating disorders.

There is a big difference between dieting to maintain a healthy weight and dieting to achieve a weight perceived to be in line with advertised models or athletes. The obsession with thinness or the desire to obtain the "perfect" body can lead to serious eating disorders that often end in health problems or death. Two common eating disorders that appear frequently on college campuses, especially among women, are anorexia nervosa (one percent are afflicted with this condition) and bulimia (four percent of college-age women suffer from this eating disorder).[3]

Anorexia nervosa is deliberate self-starvation caused by a fear of being fat. "Anorexia" means "without appetite." "Nervosa" means "of nervous origin." This disorder comes from a distorted body image caused by low self-esteem and, for perfectionists, is often a psychological plea for love. Its major symptoms are a refusal to eat, except small portions, and a denial of hunger. Anorexia nervosa results in abnormal weight loss, hair loss, sensitivity to cold, and cessation of menstruation.

With bulimia, there is an extreme preoccupation with food. The person eating usually binges in secret—and then vomits after binging. Bulimia also involves the abuse of laxatives and diet and water pills. The bulimic often exercises compulsively. If left unchecked, bulimia leads to swollen salivary glands, broken blood vessels in the eyes, discolored teeth, irritation of the esophagus, and potassium depletion which leads to life-threatening heart attacks. Bulimics are often perfectionists.

Eating disorders are a danger in a society obsessed with body image. One study showed that 80 percent of college women are dissatisfied with their appearance; another found that on one campus 91 percent of the women had attempted to control their weight through dieting; and 35 percent of "normal dieters" progress to pathological dieting.[4]

If you notice a roommate or friend with any symptoms of these disorders, tell your R.A. immediately. The person needs professional help to get at the underlying psychological condition causing the disorder. Your intervention might save a life. If *you* become preoccupied with food or exercise, go to a counselor, the school clinic, or a support group. This preoccupation can torpedo your academic career and even ruin your life. Don't be afraid to ask for help.

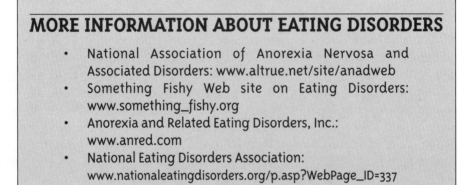

> **MORE INFORMATION ABOUT EATING DISORDERS**
>
> - National Association of Anorexia Nervosa and Associated Disorders: www.altrue.net/site/anadweb
> - Something Fishy Web site on Eating Disorders: www.something_fishy.org
> - Anorexia and Related Eating Disorders, Inc.: www.anred.com
> - National Eating Disorders Association: www.nationaleatingdisorders.org/p.asp?WebPage_ID=337

Sensible Exercise

"Whether you think you can or think you can't, you're right."
—HENRY FORD

Besides a healthy diet, committing yourself to a regular exercise program is an important ingredient for a healthy college lifestyle. Now is the time to develop an exercise and sports plan that will carry you throughout life. The secret formula for an effective exercise program is to progress slowly, getting the body gradually ready for exercise. Walking to class versus riding the campus shuttle service is a good place to start! You can later "graduate" to power walks, jogging, running, or bicycling.

Better yet, why not take advantage of the excellent recreational facilities found at most colleges today? Most are on par with private health club memberships and are included with your tuition. Spiking a volleyball, playing a hard-fought game of handball or racquetball, swimming a half-mile on a regular basis, lifting weights, or working out on the various exercise paraphernalia not only keeps your body in tip-top shape, it also is a great way to relieve stress (more on stress to follow).

Another option, especially when you determine you have the academics under control, is to participate in an intramural sport. You will likely find a variety of intramural sports in college, everything from the standards like football and basketball to more unusual sports like coed water polo played in an inner tube! Many college students enjoy participating in sports not only for the inherent value of the exercise, but for the competition, companionship, and the break in the routine.

If you are not into sports, you don't have to force yourself to be miserable just because you think you have to develop into an athlete. Why add more stress to your life? As long as you do some exercise—walking, cycling, throwing a Frisbee, golfing—it is okay to enjoy sports as a spectator. You can even ignore athletics altogether.

But *do* plan to exercise on a regular basis. Just like other busy people, you have to commit yourself to it, no matter how filled your schedule. Remember, your mind *will* function better in a well-tuned, healthy body.

SOME TIPS TO BETTER HEALTH IN COLLEGE

- Quit smoking if you are one of the 28 percent of college students who smoke.[5] If you don't smoke, don't start.
- Get enough sleep so your immune system won't wear down.
- Drink lots of water and take a daily vitamin.
- Get a vaccine shot for meningitis and hepatitis B.
- Wash your hands frequently. It's the best defense against getting germs.
- Go to the health center for the following reasons:
  → You have a nasty sore throat and fever for more than two days. You may have strep throat, which can lead to rheumatic fever and kidney problems.
  → You have a severe cough for five or six days with chest pain or shortness of breath. You may have bronchitis or even pneumonia.
  → You have chills, a fever, swollen glands, a sore throat, and profound fatigue. You may have mononucleosis.
  → You have a yellowish discoloration of the skin (jaundice), dark brown urine, loss of appetite, weakness, nausea. You may have hepatitis. Seek medical attention immediately.

Safety Consciousness

"It is better to look ahead and prepare
than to look back and regret."
—ANONYMOUS

Campus crime is a problem. "An ounce of prevention is worth a pound of cure" when it comes to being safe at college. One of three students becomes a victim, usually of a crime that other students commit and usually involving alcohol, which figures in as much as 90 percent of violent campus crimes.

How safe is your campus? Because of the 1998 Clery Act, named for Jeanne Clery, a victim of rape and murder at Lehigh University in 1986, you can find out the crime stats for your college. The Act requires colleges to report crime statistics in a timely manner. Check the Department of Education's Web site (ope.ed.gov/security) for campus crime statistics at your college or university. You can also check with the campus public safety or police department for their recent statistics. Murder, rape, robbery, aggravated assault, burglary, and auto theft do take place on and around college campuses. You need to be aware of this reality and use common sense to prevent becoming a victim. But you also need to know that most campuses are far safer than their outlying areas—whether in a downtown or major suburb. In fact, the Justice Department's Bureau of Justice Statistics found that 90 percent of the college students who were the victims of violent crime said that the crimes occurred off campus.[6]

Take some time to develop a safety plan and safety awareness. Here are some points for consideration:

- Be sure to attend freshmen orientation to gain information about safety procedures on campus. On your tour of the campus, note the location of emergency phones. Learn how to contact campus security. Program your cell phone with emergency and other important phone numbers other than 911 (e.g., RA, infirmary, counseling center.).
- Travel in groups across campus, especially at night or early morning when no one is around. Walking alone at night—especially for women—is dangerous. Use the campus escort

service, a group of paid students or volunteers who will meet you where you are and walk with you where you need to go. Always walk in well-lit areas. Be aware of your surroundings. Be wary of a stranger who asks you for directions. Keep your distance. Women, especially, should keep a can of pepper spray with them. Carry your keys in your hand so you can quickly enter your car, dorm, or apartment. Before getting into your car, watch for anyone around, under, or hiding in it. Make sure your car is in good working condition with at least a half tank of gas. Drive with your doors locked. If you think you are being followed, drive to the closest police or fire station.

- Don't go to ATMs alone at night. Avoid working or studying alone in a building at night.
- Don't jog alone, especially off campus. When you plan to go off campus, let your roommate or a friend know your plans, including when you expect to come back.
- Don't make yourself an easy target for theft. Property theft is by far the most common campus crime. Always lock your dorm door, even when you leave to go to the bathroom. Don't give your key to anyone. If you are a commuter, always lock your car. It takes only a few seconds to enter a room or car and take something. Never leave your backpack unattended. Your wallet, Ipod, cell phone, Palm Pilot, calculator, texts, and other belongings can instantly disappear. Get a sturdy U-lock for your bike. Leave irreplaceable valuables at home. Take cash and jewelry with you when you go home for weekends and vacations. Engrave your driver's license numbers preceded by your state abbreviation on expensive items (like your computer).
- Beware of developing a false sense of security. For example, do not disconnect alarms, prop open residence hall doors, or allow strangers entrance to your dorm. Double check to see that you lock your door and windows at night. It is your right to have broken locks or windows repaired immediately. Don't procrastinate getting them fixed.
- Report strangers hanging around in your dorm.
- Be alert in elevators. Stand next to the control buttons. A stranger in control of the emergency stop switch could be dangerous.

- Never drive with someone who has been drinking. Avoid alcohol yourself; too much of it impairs judgment. It also makes some students violent. Alcohol is a major factor in the majority of sexual assaults—more than 70,000 college students are victims of alcohol-related sexual assault each year.[7]

- Exercise caution when making new friends. Don't bring strangers back to your dorm room. Date in groups until you get to know well the person you are dating. Rape is the most common violent crime on college campuses. More than half of college coeds know a rape victim. Studies estimate that 25 percent of college women are victims of rape or attempted rape. Ninety percent of college women who were raped or sexually assaulted knew their rapist.[8] The most likely rapists at college are sexually aggressive male friends. Freshman women are the targets of the most rapes, with most occurring in their first three weeks at school.

- When you date, go to public places. Let your date know your standards and limits concerning alcohol and sex. Plan an exit strategy; for example, take some money along for a cab in case your date gets obnoxious and dangerous. Be careful at fraternity parties. Alcohol and peer pressure have resulted in the heinous crime of gang rape at such gatherings. Women must be especially careful about "date rape drugs" like GHB and Rohypnol. These are used to spike women's drinks before sexual assaults.

- Report all crimes or attempted crimes. If you are raped, seek medical help immediately. Involve relatives and close friends for psychological support.

- Know your dorm's fire codes and observe them. Be careful about overloading extension cords, power strips, and outlets. Do not route cords under carpets or doors. Report any code violations, for example, the use of hot plates or halogen lamps or the burning of candles or incense. Become familiar with two ways to exit your residence in case of a fire. Don't ignore fire alarms even if false first alarms are prevalent.[9]

Coping with Stress

*"Worry is like a rocking chair. It will give you something to do,
but it won't get you anywhere."*
—SOME PRACTICAL ADVICE

Stress is defined as "physical, mental, or emotional strain or tension." Not all stress is bad. An exciting trip down a raging river might be fun for one person; for another, it could be an emotional disaster. Stress triggers a flight/fight reaction as the adrenal gland produces adrenaline and cortisol to help you cope physically with the challenge. However, being in constant stress, with its steady production of stress hormones, assaults the body. It can cause headaches, stomach problems, high blood pressure, and heart disease. Poorly managed stress negatively affects the immune system, making the student much more susceptible to other diseases.

Identifying Stressors and Managing Stress

A good starting point in stress management is to locate the sources of negative stress that impede your performance. The following are typical stress producers for the average college student:
- test-taking
- paper-writing
- selecting courses
- homesickness (especially true for freshmen)
- having an obnoxious roommate
- parental expectations about grades and college major
- the lack of money
- the lack of sleep
- being ill
- coping with social pressure from friends and the demands of extracurricular activities
- having a job that chops away at study time
- being involved in a romantic relationship (or lack thereof)
- dealing with unfair, demanding professors
- carrying unrealistic self expectations

Merely naming what is stressing you can be a great help in reducing its negative influence. For example, when you know that your fear of oral reports causes you stress, you can tackle this problem directly. Practice public speaking by regularly contributing to class discussions. If term papers cause stress, seek out help in the writing lab. If your course load of 18 to 20 hours is unmanageable, find relief by dropping a course. Or, if scheduling courses stretches you to the limit, be sure to have a couple of contingency plans with alternative classes at registration time.

Here are other strategies for stress reduction and management:

- *Exercise vigorously.* Physical activity correlates well with mental acuity and psychological well being.
- *Eat well.* If you are run down physically, you'll lack the stamina to cope with stressors.
- *Prioritize.* List what is really important. Do those first. Eliminate as many nonessentials as possible.
- *Imagine the worst-case scenario.* What would you do if this really happened? Now, realistically, what are the chances that this worry will actually take place? By being mentally prepared for the worst outcome, you will be ready to handle it. After thinking it through, however, you may realize that your fears are unrealistic. Go ahead and laugh at your overactive imagination.
- *Listen to music.* Take naps. Take in a movie. Golf (even the miniature variety). Allow yourself frequent breaks from study, for example, by enjoying an occasional bull session with friends or dormmates.
- *Distinguish between working hard and being a workaholic.* Hard workers are organized and focused so they can accomplish many things. But they know when to stop and have a life other than work (study). Workaholics are disorganized, escape their problems through work, don't know when or how to relax, and are one-dimensional, that is, unable to converse about more than one topic.
- *Serve others.* Jesus taught that if you lose yourself by serving others, you'll find yourself. Participate in a college-sponsored project that helps the less fortunate. But be careful not to develop a Messiah complex by getting overly involved to the neglect of your studies.

- *Accept your humanity.* If much of your stress is self-induced ("I have to get all A's"), perhaps you are being unrealistic. Set realistic goals for yourself. Visualize restful, relaxing, and peaceful scenarios, for example, in nature. Couple this with progressive relaxation and deep-breathing exercises.
- *Get help.* Maintain a support group of friends or family and, as needed, school counselors and health professionals. Talking problems out is an effective stress reducer.
- *Pray.* More information on prayer to follow.

Depression and Suicide

Mild depression hits everyone, even college students who seem otherwise so carefree. With so many demands placed on one's time and energy, it is natural on occasion to feel sad, discouraged, and "burned out." These feelings may lead to sleeplessness, energy and appetite loss, anxiety, and feelings of emptiness. These symptoms may be more acute if a major stressor occurs: a death in your family, your parents' divorce, or a serious illness in a friend.

Realize that temporary depression is very natural. To reduce it, talk things out with a friend, exercise, get fresh air, and stimulate your senses with new surroundings. The bad times almost *always* pass. But if they don't, please visit a doctor who may discover an underlying health problem (like mono) that's making you feel bad. One word of additional warning: Never use alcohol or drugs to "drown your sorrows." They, in fact, will weaken your resolve to improve your outlook and will make you more vulnerable to negative thoughts.

When depression lasts over a longer period of time it can indicate a more serious problem. Untreated depression can lead to thoughts of suicide. Here are some sobering statistics about suicide:

- Suicide is the second leading cause of death among college-age students.
- Suicide attempts pose the greatest life-threatening danger for college women.
- The rate of suicide among young males has tripled since 1970.
- 7.5 college students out of every 100,000 take their own lives.
- Four out of five young adults who attempt suicide have given clear warnings.
- 18 to 24 year-olds think about suicide more often than any other age group, and one in twelve U.S. college students makes a suicide plan.

- The National College Health Risk Behavior Study found that 11.4 percent of students seriously consider attempting suicide.[10]

If you notice any of the following warning signs in yourself, a friend, or a roommate, express your concerns. For example, if you or a friend exhibit any of the suicide warning signs, speak up and seek help. Parents, friends, college chaplains, and suicide prevention agencies (e.g. 1-800-SUICIDE) will help you or a friend get through tough times.

SUICIDE WARNING SIGNS

- A notable change in eating and sleeping patterns
- Withdrawal from friends, family, and social activities
- A decline in academic performance
- Unusually violent or rebellious behavior
- Psychosomatic complaints
- Drug or alcohol abuse
- An unusual neglect of personal appearance
- Difficulty in concentration
- Openly talking about committing suicide or talking indirectly about "ending it all"
- A radical change in personality
- Giving away personal possessions[11]

Maintaining Spiritual Health

"Whatever, wherever I am, I can never be thrown away. If I am in sickness, my sickness may serve the Lord; in perplexity, my perplexity may serve the Lord; if I am in sorrow, my sorrow may serve the Lord. God does nothing in vain. Therefore I will trust in the Lord."
—CARDINAL JOHN HENRY NEWMAN

Medical science tells us that five nutrients—proteins, carbohydrates, fats, vitamins, and minerals—are needed for nutritional health and growth. Neglect taking any of these and your body will pay the price. The case is similar with spiritual health and growth. Neglect any five spiritual nutrients and your soul will begin to suffer: prayer, worship, community, service, and witness.

Attending to these five spiritual disciplines will help you fulfill the three basic drives that motivate college students:
- a search for meaning in life and your purpose in the universe
- a search for meaningful and sensitive relationships
- a desire to serve others.

Prayer

A Gallup poll found that nine in ten Americans pray.[12] They pray about many things: to thank God for what he has done in their lives, to seek forgiveness for specific sins, to acknowledge his greatness, and to ask for specific needs or desires.[13]

To be sure, college students pray, especially around test time! But prayer is most valuable when it is a way of life, not just a case of an emergency. Make prayer part of your daily routine as a student and you will reap great rewards. John Wesley, the father of Methodism and a great preacher, lived a strenuous, action-filled life. He once said, "Today, I have such a busy day before me that I cannot get through it with less than two hours of prayer."

Obviously, spending two hours each day in prayer would be impractical, if not impossible, for a studious collegian. But what about fifteen minutes of daily prayer? The payoff is great. Pray regularly and you will

. . . *gain a greater sense of self worth.* In prayer, you lift your mind and heart to God. When you do this, you will discover anew God's love and acceptance of *you* and come to appreciate more your tremendous worth as a person.

. . . *change for the better.* In prayer, you will be conversing—talking and listening—to the Lord, a Lord of love. He will fill your heart, mind, and soul, helping you to become a more virtuous person.

. . . *gain more energy.* Pope John Paul II is the most traveled pope in history and a man of boundless non-stop energy. Beginning his day with prayer provided the spiritual energy for him to accomplish the seemingly inhuman. Similarly, you will find prayer calming and renewing you and helping you set priorities about what is really important in your life as you complete the tasks of your day.

. . . discover healing and an increase in happiness. In prayer, God can touch and cure your emotional hurts. God forgives your sins. Through prayer you can come to a deeper realization that God is the source of true happiness, not the false gods of popularity, prettiness, prestige, possessions, straight A's, alcohol, or sex.

. . . solve some of your problems. Students worry needlessly about many things. Prayer helps you center and gain insight on how to live your life constructively as a student. To quote a popular phrase, prayer can help you "let go and let God."

A first step in *prayer basics* is to make a regular time for prayer, for example, in the break time between two classes or right after dinner before hitting the books. The time just before going to sleep is also a good time to schedule fifteen minutes of prayer.

Next, find a special place for prayer where there will be limited distractions. Some possibilities are your dorm room (when your roommate is in class), the school chapel, or a remote sofa or chair in the library. When the weather is pleasant, you can pray outdoors on a bench or while walking to a favorite locale on or near campus.

Third, use some deep breathing exercises and relaxation techniques to help you calm down. Let the hyperactivity of your day drain out of your body. There is a direct relationship between a calm body and a calm spirit. You will soon discover that a relaxing prayer time each day is a great stress reducer.

There are countless ways to pray. For example, you can read a scripture text and apply the biblical insights to your life. Or, you may find reading a book on spirituality a helpful way to focus on your relationship with God.

No matter which way you choose, I recommend that you make personal conversation with Jesus a part of your prayer experience. Become aware of Jesus' presence in your life and his care for you. Know that Jesus is your friend. Talk to him as you would your best friend about your fears, your needs, your desires. Ask him for his forgiveness for your sins, your inattentiveness, your failures to love. Thank him for the gifts of life, health, friendship, family, and your ability to do well in school.

Then, listen to Jesus. Recall the events of your past day—the people, the successes and failures, the joys and disappointments. Ask for insight as to their meaning. Reflect on what God might be telling you through these people and events. Perhaps the Lord will tell you to slow down, not to worry so much, and to trust him. Perhaps he'll challenge you to fight better the temptations of a party atmosphere so prevalent on many campuses, reassuring you that you don't have to sacrifice your integrity to fit in. Perhaps he'll comfort your troubled heart. Simply rest awhile in his company and bask in his love.

Conclude your time with God with a short resolution. For example, you might resolve to strike up a conversation with a lonely classmate. You might promise to avoid alcohol. You might pledge to call or write a younger brother or sister at home.

Make prayer a part of your college life and you will be a happier, more fulfilled student.

Worship

A national study on the religious and spiritual beliefs and practices of over 3,600 college students revealed a major drop-off in attendance at religious services during the college years. The study found that 52 percent of those surveyed reported that they frequently attended religious services their senior year of high school. This figure dropped to 29 percent by the junior year of college.[14] If your parents actively practice their faith, undoubtedly one of their major concerns may be that you will stop going to church while you are at college.

When I ask my former students why they stop going to church at college, they give many reasons: lack of time, boredom, laziness, fear of ridicule from dormmates who don't go, a bad experience with a church figure, or a problem with a given church teaching. Often the real reason is that the church represents an objective morality of right and wrong. And lax students, engaged in immoral activity like premarital sex or hedonistic drinking, do not want an authority figure like the church to challenge their newfound freedom and lifestyle.

College students also often adopt a noncommittal wariness toward the religion of their childhood. Many say things like this, "I'm not religious, but I am spiritual." They are on a search not so much for reasons that prove God's existence as to finding a spirituality where they can *meet* God.[15] They see the college years as a time to sort out their goals, aspirations, beliefs; a time to figure out who they are, where they come from and where they are going, and the meaning of existence. The college years are rightfully a time for this type of deep questioning. Nevertheless, sincere questioning is not an isolated affair. The search for the meaning of life is best begun by acknowledging a higher power, God, and seeking ways to pay respect, to honor, and to worship God in the presence of other like-minded students.

A popular myth is that because the teachings of traditional religions seem so out of step with today's secular society, religion is dead on college campuses. Not true! In fact, the counter-cultural teachings of Christ have a strong appeal to sincere college students who are honestly searching for truth amid the cacophony of voices vying for their attention. For example, religion has become one of the most popular areas of study on college campuses.

A two-year study of religiously affiliated colleges shows a significant comeback for religion on college campuses in the past decade. For example, there has been increased voluntary religious activity, renewed attention to the relations between the churches and colleges, and a growing trend of scholars who are trying to integrate their religious and spiritual beliefs into their college teaching. Membership in Campus Crusade for Christ nearly doubled in recent years. Other examples of a lively interest in religion on the campuses have been the building of interfaith chapels at schools like MIT, enrollment figures in church-affiliated colleges outpacing secular schools, and the establishment of Catholic Studies programs on many Catholic college campuses throughout the nation.[16]

Although it is difficult to come up with precise national statistics, it is true that many college students do attend worship services and find them vital to their personal growth. If you are a Catholic, you will find that some of your fellow students attend Sunday Mass out of habit, but most go simply to pray in the manner they have learned to bring them God's grace. They go to receive the Lord himself.

I would guess that Christian students of other denominations would express similar reasons for attending Sunday worship services.

Search, examine your beliefs, ask fundamental questions. But remember that these worthwhile college activities do *not* exclude worshiping with other Christian seekers around the table of faith.

Community

When he describes the university scene today, Michael J. Buckley paraphrases the "death-of-God" philosopher, Friedrich Nietzsche: "What are these universities now if not the tombs of God—monuments to the death of God within our academic culture."[17] One thing is for sure, at some time during your college career, someone will belittle, challenge, or attack your religious beliefs. My former students and my own children have told me about attacks against their beliefs.

You will find mean-spirited opposition to your beliefs coming from many sources, including professors. It is no secret that the vast majority of college professors today have a liberal political bent. The concern in this regard is that students today are not getting a balanced view on many controversial social issues since there is a natural tendency for one's personal outlook on life to influence his or her teaching.

Also, you will surely discover a secular mindset among some professors and administrators (even at Catholic or other Christian colleges) who are overtly hostile to traditional religion, especially Catholicism. A recent survey conducted by the highly respected Zogby International on behalf of the National Association of Scholars found that three-quarters of all college seniors in the survey had professors who taught them that right and wrong depends "on differences in individual values and cultural diversity." Only about a fourth of the 400 students in the randomly selected survey from colleges around the country reported that their professors taught that "there are clear and uniform standards of right and wrong by which everyone should be judged."[18] This moral relativism should neither surprise nor shock you since many of them have rejected absolute truth. The church, which represents an objective morality that teaches the existence of truth independent of one's opinion, is a threat to their comfortable, "value-free" system of education.

When your classmates notice you practicing your religion, you will probably find yourself engaged in some heated and "heavy" conversations with them as well. Many people, including those who are your age, have absorbed the conventional morality of the day that holds that all values are simply a matter of taste. They might ridicule the Christ-inspired teaching that certain behaviors are wrong despite the circumstances or a person's intentions. Don't be surprised if you find little peer support on issues like the evil of abortion or the value of self-control in matters relating to sex.

For example, a recent former student of mine, a close relative of a high-ranking government official, found himself in a sociology class at a large state university. When the topic of abortion came up, he was the *only* one of thirty students who advocated a pro-life position. Though he was under attack, he proudly told me that he stood up for life and even convinced some classmates that there were more issues to consider than the standard "pro-choice" mantra sung by his professor.

You might also meet some classmates who belong to a fundamentalist evangelical church. They will probably know the scriptures extremely well and quote them liberally, putting you on the defensive, especially if your own scriptural knowledge is a bit shaky. Some belong to churches that have a strong evangelical outreach and may even try to convert you to their religion. They will question whether you have been "born again" and claim that if you have not been (at least according to their definition of the term), then you will be condemned.

Also, you might come in contact with one or more of the cults in operation today, estimated by the American Family Foundation to be more than 1,000.[19] A Web site called CultsonCampus.com says cult recruiters seek out the most intelligent students to lend support to their particular cause. However, they often prey on lonely, depressed, and stressed-out people who are your age. Cult recruiters sometimes hang around counseling centers or cafeterias looking for students who seem isolated. Cults have a strong appeal to middle-class youths who are vulnerable and susceptible to the techniques of instant friendship, community acceptance, and the giving of out-of-proportion attention called "love bombing." Once an initiate has been hooked, the cult leaders try to get the new member to cut ties with friends and family. Though cults are not the threat on campus today that they once were, they still operate. For example, in a poll conducted by *U.Magazine*, 40 percent of the respondents reported that there are cults actively recruiting on their college campuses.[20]

In general, your best strategy for coping with these professor, peer, and cult challenges is to commit publicly to your own faith. My own children and many of my former students actually strengthened their faith when put on the defensive. Forced to reconsider more deeply our rich Catholic tradition, they became more active practitioners of faith than ever before.

However, it is important to remember that you cannot practice your religion alone. You will need a support group to help you maintain your religious identity. In fact, the biggest threat to keeping the faith comes from within yourself, rather than from professors, other students, or cults. With your newfound freedom, you will be under tremendous pressure to adopt the attitudes of your peers, especially in the areas of sex, drinking, and drugs. Always remember, though, that freedom from external restraints—like parents always looking over your shoulder—does not magically make right something that is inherently wrong.

During your first week at college, make it a top priority to contact the campus ministry office, whether you are at a state, private, or Catholic university. Campus ministry is a vital part of the church's outreach to help you develop a mature, adult faith. It is often one of the most vital organizations on campus. Its main goals are to help you belong to a vibrant community that develops you religiously and helps educate you to be a justice-loving member of Christ's body.

For Catholics, campus ministry at many state and private colleges takes the form of a Newman Club. Newman Clubs sponsor many socials as well as religious functions like weekly Mass, retreats, spiritual direction, service projects, and study groups. They are a good place to meet like-minded students who are serious about their faith but also want to share fun times together.

Service

Douglas Coupland, the coiner of the term "Generation X" (those born between 1961–1980), has the narrator of his novel *Life After God* conclude his spiritual quest this way:

> My secret is that I need God—that I am sick and can no longer make it alone. I need God to help me give, because I no longer seem to be capable of giving; to help me be kind, as I no longer seem capable of kindness; to help me love, as I seem beyond being able to love.[21]

After a long introspective look into his life and those of his friends, Coupland's hero discovered that there exists a powerful link between faith in God and the power to love, to giving, and in serving others. He is right.

A dynamic faith, sustained by a caring and loving community and nourished by prayer and the communal worship, will eventually manifest itself in some kind of loving service of others. All these elements that go into a living religion find their fulfillment in service. As the great humanitarian Albert Schweitzer said, "There is no higher religion than human service. To work for the common good is the greatest creed."

Plan to make service a part of your college experience. Perhaps you'll want to volunteer at a hospital like my daughter did or tutor disadvantaged children like many of my students have done. Maybe you will help at a local food bank or travel to Appalachia during spring break with other college students to rehabilitate depressed housing units. Or possibly you and some college friends will work for Habitat for Humanity, an organization that constructs houses for poor people, in an area near your campus. The opportunities to serve are many. Check with your campus ministry office or student life center to find various projects that are seeking volunteers.

Service has many benefits. You will grow in love and strengthen your relationship with Jesus who said: "Amen, I say to you, whatever you did for one of these least brothers of mine, you did for me" (Mt 25:40). Your faith will be authentic because it is active, committed to doing justice. And through volunteer work, you might even find your niche in life and open new career opportunities. For example, I became a teacher because of my volunteer work as a catechist at an inner city parish and at an orphanage where I taught swimming and first aid.

Finally, service will help you cope with the stresses of college life. After a lecture on mental health, the famous psychiatrist Karl Menninger was asked, "What would you tell a person who felt a nervous breakdown coming on?"

Menninger replied, contrary to his audience's expectations, "Lock up your house, go across the railway tracks, find someone in need, and then do something to help the person."

If you serve others, you will find more abundant life.

Witness

There are three kinds of people: those who make things happen, those who watch things happen, and those who don't know what is happening. Undoubtedly, you will want to be the first type, a take-charge college student who glorifies God by seeing God's presence in everything and who will use your many gifts to grow into a mature, intelligent Christian thinker.

A terrific way to maintain your Christian identity in college is simply to commit yourself to a pursuit of truth. Regardless of your course of study, when you develop your mind and hone your thinking skills, you are on a quest for Jesus who is the foundation of truth.

Committing yourself to academic excellence will make you stand out. Furthermore, a discerning mind will enable you to unmask what is shoddy in today's culture and recognize the demons that promote false values like relativism and a secularism that deifies human cleverness.

With a keen mind, you can witness to your faith by defending truth, by challenging prejudicial statements against the faith, and by questioning assumptions that unthinkingly accept the conventional morality of the day. College will present many other opportunities to proclaim your faith—informal "rap sessions" with classmates, papers you write for philosophy and other classes, conversations with your roommate. Sharing your faith with others will strengthen it and may even help lead others to embrace it.

What if you feel unprepared to explain your faith, perhaps due to an inadequate religious education? Here's the advice I have offered my own students and children: You can take a theology course from a faith-filled professor, join a campus ministry study group, keep handy a copy of a catechism, and read some good introductory theology books on your religion. Adopt these and other ideas to help you grow in knowledge of your faith so you can witness it to others.

Conclusion

I want to thank you for reading this book. I hope some of the tips will help make your first few months at college a little easier. Congratulations again on beginning this exciting part of your life's journey. I will keep you in my prayers. I hope God will bless you with much wisdom and love.

Yours in Christ,
Mike Pennock

End Notes

Introduction: Fresh Start

1. U.S. Department of Education, "Changes in College Completion Rates," from "College for All? Is There Too Much Emphasis on Getting a 4-year College Degree?" January 1999. www.ed.gov/pubs/CollegeForAll/completion.html (5 January 2004).
2. Jonathan Whitbourne, "The Dropout Dilemma: One in Four College Freshmen Drop Out. What is Going on Here? What Does It Take to Stay In?" *Careers and Colleges*, March 2002. Located in LookSmart, c. 2002 EM Guild, Inc. and c. 2002 Gale Group. www.findarticles.com/cf_0/m0BTR/4_22/84599442/p1/article.jhtm (5 January 2004).

One: Counting Down the Days

1. A summary of various college institutional studies. Found at Randall S. Hansen, Ph.D., "Your First Year of College: 25 Tips to Help You Survive and Thrive Your Freshmen Year and Beyond," QuintCareers.Com www.quintcareers.com/first-year_success.html (5 January 2004).
2. "Catholic Higher Education: What Happened?—A Parent's Lament," *Commonweal*, April 9, 1993, p. 15.
3. Laurie Andersen, "Getting into College," Penguin Group (USA), 2003. www.penguinputnam.com/static/packages/us/razorbill2003/college.html (5 January 2004).
4. Both quotes found at the Web site Aphorism Galore! www.ag.wastholm.net/home (5 January 2004).
5. Anthony De Mello, S.J., *Awareness* (New York: Doubleday, 1990), p. 76.
6. John Powell, S.J., *Happiness Is an Inside Job* (Allen, TX: Tabor Publishing, 1989).
7. Tamar Lewin, "As Textbook Prices Skyrocket, Students Look for Alternatives," *New York Times* article reprinted in the *Cleveland Plain Dealer*, September 16, 2003, p. A-1, A-10.
8. *Cleveland Plain Dealer*, September 4, 2003, p. F8.
9. Nellie Mae, "2001 Credit Card Usage Analysis," April 2002 www.nelliemae.com/library/research_9.html (5 January 2004).

Two: The First Weeks on Campus

1. Robert Fulghum, *It Was on Fire When I Lay Down on It* (New York: Ivy Books, Ballantine, 1989), pp. 78–79.
2. Found at Famous Quotations www.famousquotations.com/asp/search.asp?keyword=patience (23 September 2003).
3. Private correspondence with friend and former student, Danny O'Malley.
4. Cited in Sherrie Nist, Ph.D. and Jodi Patrick Holschuh, Ph.D., *College Rules! How to Study, Survive, and Succeed in College* (Berkeley: Ten Speed Press, 2002), p. 33. [This is an excellent book to help you learn how to study in college.]
5. "College Freshmen Can Combat Homesickness, Says University of Dayton Counselor" www.udayton.edu/news/nr/081998.html (6 January 2004).

6. Barry Guinagh, "Homesickness in the Freshman Year," *Journal of the Freshman Year Experience*, 4 (No. 1, 1992): 111–120. [The study also discovered that females experience homesickness more than males.]
7. Jonathan Whitborne, "The Dropout Dilemma: One in Four College Freshmen Drop Out. What Is Going on Here? What Does It Take to Stay In?" *Careers & Colleges*, March 2002, p. 26.
8. TheHometownChannel.com, "College Freshmen Suffer from 'Friendsickness'": Researcher Urges Universities to Help Students Adjust, August 11, 2003 www.local6.com/family/2395777/detail.html (6 January 2004).
9. Debra Humphreys, "The Impact of Diversity on College Students: The Latest Research," Association of American Colleges and Universities' Diversity Web www.diversityweb.org/research_and_trends/research_evaluation_impact/ benefits_of_diversity/impact_of_diversity.cfm (6 January 2004).
10. *Ibid.*
11. Patrick Combs, *Major in Success*, 4th edition (Berkeley, Ten Speed Press, 2003).
12. If you want to read his other rules to live by, see Robert Fulghum, *All I Really Need to Know I Learned in Kindergarten* (New York: Ivy Books, 1988), pp. 4–5.

Three: Hitting the Books

1. This really happened to a student who told her story in *Reader's Digest*, October 1995, p. 113.
2. As reported by Sherrie Nast, Ph.D. and Jodi Patrick Holschun, Ph.D. in *College Rules! How to Study, Survive, and Succeed in College* (Berkeley, CA: Ten Speed Press, 2002), p. 49.
3. John L. Holland, *Making Vocational Choices: A Theory of Careers* (Englewood Cliffs, NJ: Prentice-Hall, 1973).
4. National Survey of Student Engagement 2003 Annual Report, *Converting Data into Action: Expanding the Boundaries of Institutional Improvement*, pp. 13, 33 www.iub.edu/~nsse/2003_annual_report/ (7 January 2004).
5. This is a widely adapted version of Professor Francis P. Robinson's SQ3R method created in World War II to help servicemen learn more effectively in accelerated university courses.

Four: The Challenges and Dilemmas of College Life

1. Christopher F. Monte, *Merlin: The Sorcerers' Guide to Survival in College* (Belmont, CA: Wadsworth Publishing Co., 1990), pp. 23–49.
2. Eric A. Storch and Jason B. Storch, "Fraternities, Sororities, and Academic Dishonesty," *College Student Journal*, Vol. 36, June 2002, 247f. Available from Academic Search Elite [database on-line] search.epnet.com/direct.asp?an=7169654&db=aph (Boston, MA: EBSCO Publishing, accessed 8 January 2004).
3. Maureen Sirhal, "Fraternities on the Rocks," *Policy Review*, February-March 2000, No. 99, published by the Heritage Foundation www.policyreview.org/ feb00/sirhal.html (8 January 2004).
4. Leon R. Kass, "The End of Courtship," *The Public Interest*, Number 126. Winter 1997, found online at www.thepublicinterest.com (8 January 2004).

5. Institute for American Values, "Hooking Up, Hanging Out, and Hoping for Mr. Right: College Women on Dating and Mating Today," 2001. Retrieved 17 November 2003 from LexisNexis Database (Current Issues Universe, R071-7) on the World Wide Web: www.lexisnexis.com/ciuniv. [Most of the findings in this section of the chapter come from this study.]

6. Gary Gately, "College Kids Ignore Risks of Unsafe Sex," ABC News Online, 3 September 2003 abcnews.go.com/sections/living/Healthology/HS_college-sex_030903.html (8 January 2004).

7. Gary Gately, "Sex on Campus: Risky Business," 4 woman.gov—The National Women's Health Information Center www.4woman.gov/news/nov071.htm (8 January 2004).

8. U.S. Department of Health and Human Services, "HIV/AIDS Statistics," Facts and Figures, January 2004 www.niaid.nih.gov/factsheets/aidsstat.htm (8 January 2004).

9. "Substance Use and Risky Sexual Activity." National Center on Addiction and Substance Abuse, Columbia University. (2002). Retrieved 8 January 2004 from LexisNexis Database (Current Issues Universe, U006-27) on the World Wide Web: www.lexisnexis.com/ciuniv.

10. Cited by Heather Koerner, "College Students Turn Pro-Life," *Boundless Webzine* www.boundless.org/2002_2003/features/a0000703.html (8 January 2004).

11. National Institute on Alcohol Abuse and Alcoholism, "College Students and Drinking," Alcohol Alert No. 29, Bethesda, MD: U.S. Department of Health and Human Services, 1998.

12. Reported by the Center for Science in the Public Interest's Alcohol Policies Project, "Fact Sheet: Binge Drinking on College Campuses" www.cspinet.org/booze/collfact1.htm (8 January 2004).

13. United Press International, "Task Force: Binge Drinking Worse Than Ever," April 9, 2002, Retrieved 8 January 2004 from SIRS Discoverer on the Web www.sirs.com.

14. "Quick Hits: Sex in the News," *Contemporary Sexuality*, Vol. 36, No. 5, May 2002. Retrieved 8 January 2004 from Academic Search Premier database search. epnet.com/direct.asp?an=6701371&db=aph.

15. Center for Science in the Public Interest's Alcohol Policies Project. www.lexisnexis.com/ciuniv.

16. BuddyT, "Acute Alcohol Poisoning," alcoholism.about.com/library/nosearch/n000723.htm (8 January 2004).

17. See, for example, Michael Wilbon's "It's a Long Descent into Madness," *The Washington Post*, 5 March 2003, Sports section, D01. Found online with the TOPICsearch database search.epnet.com/direct.asp?an=WPT304118557903&db=tth (8 January 2004).

18. Statistics on cheating cited by Plagiarism.org www.plagiarism.org/plagiarism_stats.html (8 January, 2004).

19. Quoted in Tony Castle, *'Quotations for All Occasions'* (London: Marshall-Pickering, 1989), p. 167.

Five: Keeping Physically and Spiritually Fit

1. "Combatting the Infamous Freshman 15! Tupperware Poll Shows More Than Half of Those Who Attend College Change Eating Habits" PR Newswire, August 19, 2003 www.findarticles.com/cf_0/m4PRN/2003_August_19/106681849/p1/article.jhtml (9 January 2004).

2. The Federal Citizen Information Center, "The Food Guide Pyramid."

3. Anorexia and Related Eating Disorders, Inc., "Statistics: How Many People Have Eating Disorders?" ANRED Web site www.anred.com/stats.html (9 January 2004).

4. National Eating Disorders Association, "Statistics: Eating Disorders and Their Precursors," NEDA Web site www.nationaleatingdisorders.org/p.asp?WebPage_ID=325&Profile_ID=41138 (9 January 2004).

5. "Smoking on College Campuses," Action on Smoking and Health Web site's summary of a March, 2001, Harvard study www.no-smoking.org/march01/03-26-01-3.html (9 January 9, 2004).

6. Safe Campuses Now Web site, "Statistics," www.safecampusesnow.org/Statistics.htm (9 January 2004).

7. "College Crime Stats-101," found at CollegeSAFE.com www.collegesafe.com/college_crime.htm (9 January 2004).

8. *Ibid*.

9. More fire safety tips can be found at Underwriters Laboratories, Inc., "Dorm Room Safety 101," New Release, August 27, 2002 www.ul.com/media/newsrel/nr082702d.html (9 January 2004).

10. The JED Foundation, "Suicide Facts" jedfoundation.org/suicide.php (9 January, 2004).

11. National Mental Health Association, "Finding Hope and Help: College Student & Depression Pilot Initiative Fact Sheets" www.nmha.org/camh/college/fact_sheets.cfm#suicide (9 January 9, 2004).

12. The Gallup Organization, "As Nation Observes National Day of Prayer, 9 in 10 Pray" www.gallup.com/subscription/?m=f&c_id=10494 (9 January 2004).

13. Barna Research Online, "Faith Commitment" www.barna.org/cgi-bin/PageCategory.asp?CategoryID=19 (9 January 2004).

14. "Most College Students Value Religion, Study Says," Los Angeles Times, November 29, 2003. This report of UCLA's Higher Education Research Institute's study found at HeraldNet www.heraldnet.com/Stories/03/11/29/17803746.cfm (5 December 2003).

15. See Arthur Schwartz, "Growing Spiritually During the College Years," originally published in Liberal Education, Fall 2001, Vol. 87, No. 4. Found online at Looksmart www.findarticles.com/cf_dls/m0NKR/4_87/88581394/p1/article.jhtml (9 January 2004).

16. Kathleen A. Mahoney, John Schmalzbauer, James Youniss, "Religion: A Comeback on Campus," Liberal Education, Fall 2001, Vol. 87, No. 4, Association of American Colleges and Universities www.findarticles.com/cf_dls/m0NKR/4_87/88581395/p1/article.jhtml (9 January 2004).

17. Michael J. Buckley, "The Catholic University and Its Inherent Promise," America, May 1993, p. 14.

18. Lawrence Morahan, "College Professors Spread Moral Relativism," CNSNews.com, July 9, 2002. Reprinted from NewsMax.com www.newsmax.com/archives/articles/2002/7/8/182116.shtml (9 January 2004).

19. Andrew J. Pulskamp, 'Are Cults Working Your College Campus?" U.Magazine, Colleges.com www.colleges.com/Umagazine/articles.taf?category=campusclips&article=campuscults (9 January 2004).

20. Ibid.

21. Douglas Coupland, Life After God (New York: Pocket Books, 1994), p. 359.

Michael Pennock, a master teacher for 36 years, saw thousands of students off to college. He received letters, e-mails, phone calls, and visits from his former students telling him of the successes and stresses of college life.

His unique perspective on the college experience also includes getting four of his own children ready for college.

God...Any Time, Any Place
The Many Ways College Students Pray
Pegge Bernecker

The majority of college students say they want to pray, but their busy schedules challenge them to find time to cultivate their spiritual lives.
God...Any Time, Any Place shares how, when, where, and why of hundreds of college students from around the nation who recognize the importance of maintaining a regular prayer practice and have found ways to do it. By following the examples in this book, readers are encouraged to consider their own prayer practice. Each chapter contains several follow-up reflection questions to give readers a sense of how to proceed, either through individual reflection or through group sharing or both.
ISBN: 1-59471-019-8 / 128 pages / $9.95

Sacred Space
The Prayer Book 2005
Jesuit Communication Centre, Ireland

Sacred Space: The Prayer Book 2005 is the first annual prayer guide inspired by the hugely successful interactive website, www.sacredspace.ie. Both offer a way to reflect and pray each day of the year, a time to quietly connect with God, a time to be consoled, healed, challenged, and transformed.
Sacred Space offers a daily selection from Scripture, followed by points of inspiration to help us think about the passage and make it relevant to our daily lives. Each week centers on a theme, and we are encouraged to reflect each day upon six stages of prayer specially created for the weekly theme.
And because a new **Sacred Space** will be available every year, your prayer life will continue to grow.
ISBN: 1-59471-030-9 / 384 pages / $12.95

KEYCODE: F0A0105000000